PRAYER
AND
TEMPERAMENT

Different Prayer Forms
for
Different Personality Types

BY
Chester P. Michael
and
Marie C. Norrisey

THE OPEN DOOR, INC.
P. O. Box 855
Charlottesville, Virginia 22902
(804) 293-5068

Library of Congress Catalog Card Number: 84-61839
ISBN: 0-940136-01-5

Fourth Printing
Published by: THE OPEN DOOR INC.
P.O. Box 855
Charlottesville, Virginia 22902
(804) 293-5068

Printed in the United States of America by
Wm. Byrd Press, Richmond, Virginia

In grateful acknowledgment to all those who participated in the 1982 *Prayer and Temperament Project*. Without their enthusiastic support this project could not have been undertaken.

TABLE OF CONTENTS

INTRODUCTION

During the past decade with its emphasis on personal growth and fulfillment, a good amount of interest has been generated concerning the relationship between one's temperament or personality and one's style of prayer and spirituality. During many workshops, seminars, retreat experiences, and in the spiritual direction of numerous persons, the authors have been experimenting with the theory that there is a relationship between one's temperament and the kind of prayer or spirituality that is practiced by different persons. Furthermore, in 1982, 457 persons from all over the country were recruited to engage in a year-long project to discern the value of various prayer forms for the different psychological types of human personality. Of those taking part in the project, 98% testified to the value of choosing a method of prayer which was compatible to their temperament.

Everyone involved in the Prayer Project took the Myers-Briggs Type Indicator (MBTI) to determine their personality type and introduced by way of recommendation to the Kiersey-Bates Temperament Sorter (pp. 5-ll, *Please Understand Me*), which is not as accurate but is quick and very helpful. Others in the Project also took the Gray-Wheelwright Jungian Type Survey (Society of Jungian Analysts, San Francisco, CA), which is especially helpful for discerning one's Dominant and Inferior Functions. The method used by the various personality tests to determine one's type is to ask a series of questions to determine preferences of how one views and perceives reality and how one acts and makes judgments.

People who have taken either the Myers-Briggs Type Indicator (MBTI) or the shorter Kiersey Temperament Sorter are absolutely amazed at the accuracy with which the portraits describe the temperament and personality of the individual. It almost appears as though someone has been following each of us around and is describing our own individual personality instead of giving a general description of one of sixteen types of personality. These indicators so accurately describe one's characteristic or habitual inclination that we strongly recommend that every husband and wife, every parent and child, every prospective bride and groom, every member of a staff or working group should take the MBTI and share the findings with the other members of the group. Such sharing would probably eliminate 50% of the misunderstandings which normally arise in marriages, families, and other close relationships or working groups. Not only will we understand ourselves better and why we perceive reality and make judgments and decisions the way we do, but we will also understand why others see reality differently and arrive at decisions at variance with our own. General knowledge of the differences in human temperament should help to overcome much intolerance and many misunderstandings in human society.

In addition to the wonderful benefits of self-understanding and mutual understanding in marriage, family life, school, office, factory, and other groupings, many of us have discovered another tremendous benefit from knowing something about type and temperament. We are realizing that there is a different type of prayer and spirituality that is appropriate to each of the four basic temperaments and perhaps also even for the sixteen different types of personality. The research of Briggs-Myers and Kiersey-Bates was done in the secular fields. So far little extensive research has been done in the application of these findings to prayer and spirituality. However, as a result of the research done by the authors of this book, certain conclusions concerning methods of prayer for the different types and temperaments have emerged. Those who have followed the suggestions offered by us during the Prayer Project and in spiritual direction have found real help in developing a more meaningful prayer life which in turn spurs on their spiritual growth.

One of the great tragedies during the past several centuries is that we have been more or less forced by training into a form of prayer or spirituality that was indeed a proper method for one particular temperament. Unfortunately that temperament belonged only to a small number of those who took seriously the need for prayer. One was given the impression that this traditional method of prayer was the best method for everyone. When it did not work, the conclusion was that there was something wrong with the person rather than with the method. Therefore, many of us decided that we were not destined for sanctity since the recommended way of spirituality could not be achieved, even with supreme and heroic effort. The result was that many good people gave up prayer altogether or went through the motions of praying without any real interior effect or benefit.

In our 1982 survey of the relationship between temperament and prayer there were participants in all sixteen of the individual types of human personality. 75% of the participants were women, 25% were men. Of these 44 were clergymen of various church affiliations, 84 were women of different religious communities, the rest were lay persons. Throughout the year regular reports of their reactions to the different prayer suggestions and other material, which we sent them, were returned to us. Only 2% of the more than 400 men and women taking part in the project indicated they derived no value from the suggestions. Our conclusion, based on questionnaire returns, was that this 2% had reached a higher state of prayer and contemplation which depends directly on the inspiration of the Holy Spirit. Therefore, suggestions given herewith are not meant for those who are in the unitive way of the higher mansions of prayer and passive contemplation as described by St. Teresa of Avila. Aside from this very small group, participants in the prayer project reported 95% of the prayer suggestions given to them had value for their type. With the help of the criticisms and suggestions given by the participants, we have attempted to correct any inaccuracies that had existed in our theory concerning the relationship between temperament and particular forms of prayer.

Adapting the findings of the MBTI to the amelioration of our spiritual life is one of a number of tools which can help us in our growth toward wholeness and holiness. Like any tool, however, it is not universally applicable. There will be a number of persons who do not fit into the molds suggested by the four basic temperaments and the sixteen personality types. This is typical of the human situation where every person is unique and somewhat different from every other human being. Some of us are more unique than others. This does not mean that there is anything wrong with us. We simply have to work a little harder to find the tools and means that will fit our particular situation. Those who are able to pray without the benefit of a knowledge of temperament should continue to follow the path that works best for them; but what we are saying is that a very large majority, perhaps 90%, of those who are introduced to the theory of temperament or type do find that this knowledge becomes an excellent tool to help them pray better. By learning their type with its good attributes and shortcomings, they have been helped to understand their strengths and limitations and how to use in prayer those parts of their personality which do not function naturally or easily.

Everything said in this book about the relationship of temperament and prayer needs to be taken with certain reservations. The conclusions drawn are never to be taken absolutely. They are only somewhat true and somewhat applicable. The rule to follow is to try out the suggestions. If they work for you and help deepen your prayer life and your relationship with God, then make use of them. Since most persons who have tried to follow these suggestions have found them helpful to their prayer life, the hope is that you too will experience some benefit from them. Think of them as "tools" that are meant to assist your efforts to make contact with God, to maintain this relationship, and to deepen it through your prayer. God can and frequently does directly intervene in our lives in His own way. We must keep ourselves open to whatever helps we can get from every possible source. The study and knowledge of temperament and type is one of these helps.

In Appendix I we give a brief description of the four pairs of preferences which determine the particular temperament and personality to which one belongs. Those who do not have easy access to either the MBTI or the Kiersey-Bates Temperament Sorter may use this Appendix to determine their temperament or personality type. Those who already know their MBTI scores may use this Appendix to check the validity of the type given by these scores.

Appendix II, in our estimation, is one of the most valuable parts of this book. It gives the prayer suggestions that we have found helpful for each of the sixteen personality types and also suggestions on how to recognize one's shadow and develop its potential through prayer.

In Appendix III we have given a glossary of terms and expressions used in this book that come from the areas of prayer, temperament, and depth psychology. Rather than attempt to explain each new term we have used, we have put their definitions in this Appendix in the back of the book. Please refer frequently to this glossary of terms until you become familiar with the vocabulary used in this book. Appendix IV will give the temperament range of those participating in the 1982 Prayer Project.

A brief summary of the book's contents is as follows. Chapter One of the book gives an overview of the history and development of the theory of temperament followed by a brief description of how temperament has affected the development of prayer and spirituality throughout the Christian Era. A chapter is then devoted to each of the five types of personal prayer which the Christian tradition has developed over the centuries. How each temperament might use its Shadow and Inferior Function in prayer is then explored. Finally, the theory of temperament is applied to public prayer or liturgy, especially the Eucharist.

CHAPTER ONE

AN OVERVIEW

THE HISTORY AND DEVELOPMENT OF THE
THEORY OF TEMPERAMENT

For at least twenty-five centuries human beings have been aware of certain distinct differences in human temperament or personality. Around 450 B. C., Hippocrates, the Father of Medical Science, divided the human race into four temperaments. His theory was that the cause of the differences in human personality was an inbalance of the four "humors" or secretions of the heart, liver, lungs, and kidneys. He designated the temperaments according to these four secretions: Sanguine (blood from the heart); Choleric (yellow bile from the liver); Phlegmatic (phlegm from the lungs); Melancholic (black bile from the kidneys). Galen, the greatest of the Greco-Roman physicians, took up the theory of Hippocrates and amplified it by showing that differences of temperament were something positive rather than a negative inbalance of bodily secretions. In the sixteenth century a Swiss physician, theologian, and alchemist named Paracelsus further elaborated the theory of four basic temperaments by using the four elements of water, earth, air, and fire to distinguish their different traits.

The division of human personalities into four basic temperaments continued to be the traditional theory until Carl G. Jung published his study of personality types in 1920. By positing two attitudes toward life (Extraversion and Introversion) and four operating functions (Sensation, Intuition, Thinking, Feeling), Jung arrived at a total of eight different psychological types. His findings were published in English in 1923 under the title, *Psychological Types*. In this country Katharine C. Briggs and her daughter, Isabel Briggs Myers, took up the findings of Jung and after forty years of research and amplification came out in 1962 with the Myers-Briggs Type Indicator by which sixteen distinct types of personality could be distinguished. After her mother's death and all through her life, Isabel Briggs Myers continued her work with human temperament; and her findings and conclusions were published in *Gifts Differing* in 1980, just before her death.

Meanwhile, David Kiersey, a clinical psychologist working in California, further expanded on the insights of Jung and the Myers-Briggs team and in 1976 published with Marilyn Bates the book, *Please Understand me*. From the sixteen types of personality identified by Isabel Myers, Kiersey isolated four basic temperaments of human behavior. Each of these four temperaments has four sub-types following the sixteen types demarcated by Isabel Myers and her mother.

The Four Pairs of Preferences

E-I
S-N
T-F
J-P

Both the Briggs-Myers team and the Kiersey-Bates team use four pairs of preferences — Extraversion-Introversion, Sensing-Intuition, Thinking-Feeling, Judging and Perceiving — to arrive at the sixteen distinct types of human personality. Two of these pairs of preferences (E-I and J-P) are termed attitudes, while the other two pairs (S-N and T-F) are called functions. Isabel Myers assigned letters to each of these eight choices: E for Extraversion, I for Introversion, S for Sensing, N for Intuition, T for Thinking, F for Feeling, J for Judging, and P for Perceiving. The MBTI (Myers Briggs Type Indicator) gives the relative strength of each person's preference.

According to the temperament theory of Jung and Briggs-Myers everyone has some ability in all of the choices, but most people show a marked tendency to use one side of each of the four pairs of preferences and neglect to use the other side except when necessary. This results in a more or less habitual use of one side of each pair of preferences in all our conscious behavior and conscious life and the relegation of the opposite side to the realm of the unconscious. This opposite side is called an inferior function or attitude or sometimes "the shadow". This attribute is available for use in our conscious life but requires considerably more psychic energy to activate than does the conscious habitually-used side. The sixteen types, designated by the particular four letters which comprise our habitual, conscious choices in the four pairs of preferences, are: ESTJ, ISTJ, ESTP, ISTP, ESFJ, ISFJ, ESFP, ISFP, ENTJ, INTJ, ENTP, INTP, ENFJ, INFJ, ENFP, INFP.

The first pair of preferences (E-I) shows one's preferential attitude toward relationship with the world. The Extravert relies primarily on the outer world of people and things to receive the needed psychic energy and enthusiasm for living. The Introvert relies primarily upon the inner world of ideas, concepts, and spirit in order to find the needed energy to live. Every human being can be extraverted or introverted depending upon the occasion, but most people definitely prefer to be one more than the other.

The second and third pairs of preferences (S-N, T-F) refer to the four basic psychological functions which everyone uses for perceiving new data and in making the necessary judgment or decision for acting upon this data. The Perceiving Functions, Sensing and Intuition, are the second pair of preferences; and the Judging Functions, Thinking and Feeling, the third pair of preferences.

The Perceiving Functions, Sensing and Intuition, are used to gather the data and information which we use in order to carry on our life. Sensing makes use of the five bodily senses of seeing, hearing, touching, tasting, and smelling to make contact with the actual state of affairs as it exists in the here and now. The Sensing Function is primarily concerned with gathering data of the physical world in which we live, including our own body and all outside, physical, material bodies. In general, the Sensing Function furnishes us with the data of the actual situation in which we presently find ourselves. Yet, by means of symbols, the Sensing Function is also able to make contact with the inner world of spirit. For example, it tells us whether we are happy or sad, enthusiastic or depressed, peaceful or disturbed. Through a symbol-making process, the Sensing Function senses the presence of God and the transcendental level of reality as distinct from the physical world.

The Intuitive Function perceives the great potential and new possibilities in both the external physical world and the inner world of spirit and ideas. As the creative, visionary function, Intuition makes it possible for us to create new things or bring about improvements in the present situation. While the Sensing Function is primarily concerned with the external physical world and only secondarily involved with the inner world of spirit, the Intuitive Function is primarily concerned with the inner world and only secondarily concerned with the outer world. Thus the two Perceiving Functions are complementary, and both are needed for a full and balanced life. However, depending upon individual temperament, each of us has a tendency to favor one way of perceiving rather than the other.

The two Judging Functions, Thinking and Feeling, are used to make the necessary judgments and decisions as to what we will do with the data which has been furnished by the Perceiving Functions. Both make value judgments but arrive at them through different methods. The Thinking Function uses the mind and intellect to arrive at a judgment or decision by following a logical, methodical method. The Feeling Function uses the heart and inner experiences of personal relationship and love to arrive at its judgment and decision. The Thinking Function is more objective and impersonal, emphasizing justice, objective truth, fairness. The Feeling Function is more subjective and personal, emphasizing the personal values and the effects which the decision or judgment will have on the persons involved, whether they be oneself or others. In making good judgments and decisions, we need to use both the Thinking Function and the Feeling Function, but each of us is inclined to give more weight to one function rather than to the other, making it one of the four determining factors of our temperament or personality.

Of these four functions — Sensing, Intuition, Thinking, Feeling — one will be the Dominant Function upon which a person relies more heavily than any of the others. The opposite of the Dominant Function is called the Inferior Function because it is undifferentiated and more or less deeply buried in the unconscious. Another function is called the Auxiliary Function because it is the main help upon which the Dominant Function relies to carry out its particular work. The opposite of the Auxiliary Function is simply called the third or Tertiary Function. If the Dominant is a Perceiving Function (Sensing or Intuition), then the Auxiliary will always be a Judging Function (Thinking or Feeling). Vice-versa is also true. If the Dominant Function is a Judging Function, the Auxiliary will always be a Perceiving Function. In the order of ascendancy, then, it would be Dominant, Auxiliary, Tertiary, and Inferior.

In her study of human personalities Isabel Myers discovered an interesting phenomenon. Extraverts use their Dominant Function when dealing with the external world and rely on their Auxiliary Function when dealing with the inner world of ideas, concepts, spirit. On the other hand, Introverts use their Dominant Function in the inner world, and depend upon their Auxiliary Function when they deal with the external world. For this reason, Introverts are much more difficult to get to know. Since they do not show their Dominant

Function to the external world but show their Auxiliary, it is difficult to type their temperament accurately.

Isabel Myers and her mother also discovered that each one of us shows a definite preference for using either the Perceiving Functions or the Judging Functions when relating to the world. Therefore, they added a fourth pair of preferences and called them Judging and Perceiving. Those who prefer using the Judging Functions, Thinking and Feeling, when relating to the world around them, are called the "J" people. They give their main attention and concern to making judgments and decisions about how things and persons in the world should act. Those who prefer using their Perceiving Functions, Sensing and Intuition, in relating to the outside world are called "P" people. They are primarily concerned with getting more data and information without coming to closure. The "J" persons are quite structured and decisive in their approach to life. The "P" persons are usually more flexible and open-ended. They usually are slower in arriving at a decision than the "J" people. The "P" person is less structured and less time-conscious than the "J" person.

Please refer to Appendix I for more information on the characteristics of these different functions and attitudes as they relate and combine to form a particular type or temperament.

Function Theory versus Temperament Theory

Isabel Myers and those who have followed her lead are primarily concerned about the relationship of the different functions in regard to temperament. David Kiersey, while acknowledging the value and place of the functions in determining temperament, has sought to bring the insights of Jung and Briggs-Myers into accord with the very ancient and constant tradition of four basic temperaments. To do this he has been concerned more with the external behavior of the different types rather than how each type functions. Thus he has arrived at a theory of four basic temperaments: Sensing-Judging (SJ), Sensing-Perceiving (SP), Intuition-Thinking (NT), and Intuiion-Feeling (NF). Note that in this classification, Kiersey uses only two pairs of preferences in determining the basic temperament. When the Perceiving Function is Sensing, he uses the fourth pair of preferences, J or P. When the Perceiving Function is Intuition, he uses the third pair of preferences, T or F. Arriving at this conclusion by the inductive method of studying the four typical pathological cases of hysteria, depression, compulsion, and impulsive behavior, he then discovered that the behavior of normal, healthy people also fell into these same four categories or temperaments.

The difference of opinion seems to arise from the two different points of view with which we can approach human personality. If we approach it from the aspect of outward behavior, then the use of the four basic temperaments described by David Kiersey is quite accurate. If we approach it from the angle of how the inner functions operate, then the descriptions of temperaments and types of personality given by Isabel Briggs Myers seems to fit the situation best. It is not a case of either/or, but of both/and. In this book we have attempted to use the insights of both Myers and Kiersey. To do so, we have made a distinction between spirituality and prayer. Spirituality concerns our behavior in the three basic relationships: with God, with our neighbor, and with ourselves. Prayer concerns the inner workings of the specific relationship with God.

Kiersey cites four Greek gods for their attributes and names them as the patrons of these four basic temperaments: Epimethean (SJ), Dionysian (SP), Promethean (NT), and Apollonian (NF). These four basic temperaments resemble somewhat the four temperaments of Hippocrates. SJ might also be termed Melancholic; SP—Sanguine; NT—Phlegmatic; NF—Choleric. In this book we have used the names of four well-known saints to identify these four temperaments and their appropriate spirituality. We have called the SJ temperament and spirituality Ignatian (St. Ignatius of Loyola); the SP, Franciscan (St. Francis of Assisi); the NT, Thomistic (St. Thomas Aquinas); and the NF, Augustinian (St. Augustine of Hippo).

Relationship of Temperament to Prayer and Spirituality

All indicators point to a close relationship between our innate temperament and the type of prayer best suited to our needs. Introverts will prefer a form of prayer different from Extraverts. Intuitives approach God from a point of view different from Sensers. Feelers pray in a different way from Thinkers. Judging persons want structure in their prayer life, while Perceiving persons want flexibility. As we grow in maturity and learn to make good use of all our abilities in functioning and relating, our prayer life should become richer. While we may still prefer the type of prayer that matches our natural temperament, we should familiarize ourselves with the other forms of prayer that have been developed over the centuries.

As far as the relation of prayer to the four functions is concerned, our recommendation is that, for the most part, we should use our Dominant and Auxiliary Functions in our daily prayer periods. Since we have the most facility with these two functions, prayer will not become a burden if we rely primarily upon them; but we should also try to use our Tertiary Function frequently. The Inferior Function should not be entirely neglected in prayer since, according to Jung, this is the function which the unconscious uses most often to reveal the riches of the inner life of the spirit. Using this fourth, undeveloped function requires much more psychic energy than does using the Dominant and Auxiliary Functions. Therefore, it would be a mistake to attempt to activate this inferiorly developed function in all of our prayer periods. For most people, if this were attempted, prayer would become too much of a burden and most likely would be abandoned. Rather, we should wait for those more leisurely moments in our life when we have lots of time to muster the extra psychic energy needed to use the Inferior Function. If used then, some of the deepest and most meaningful faith experiences may occur. The Tertiary Function acts somewhat after the manner of the Inferior Function and somewhat after the manner of the Auxiliary Function. Therefore, it can be activated with less effort than the Inferior Function but still not as easily as the Auxiliary or Dominant Functions. In Appendix II, with the prayer recommendations for the sixteen types of personality, you will also find the Dominant, Auxiliary, Tertiary, and Inferior Functions for each of these sixteen types.

We are able to make contact with God and experience grace through all four of the psychological functions. Each of these functions has a transcendent dimension which enables us to get in touch with God and the spiritual, transcendental values of life. Some examples of these transcendentals are love, truth, beauty, goodness, unity, justice, life, adoration, worship, reverence, gratitude, and contrition. These are the values which we try to actualize in prayer and through prayer energize in our conscious life. Through the activation of the transcendent dimension of each of the four functions we receive the psychic energy necessary to perform our daily duties, make contact with God in prayer, discern God's will, and receive the grace to fulfill our destiny on earth. (See Chapter Eight for a further explanation of the transcendent dimension and its relationship to the shadow and prayer.)

Prayer touches and influences us only to the extent that it succeeds in activating the transcendent dimension of one or more of the four functions of Sensing, Intuition, Thinking, and Feeling. The different prayer forms described in this book will enable one to energize the transcendent dimension of the different functions. Our recommendation is that one should use all five of the methods described in order to vitalize all four functions and thus create a proper balance in our ordinary life, in our prayer life, and in our relationship with God. By practicing all five of the methods of prayer described, one will discover the particular method or methods that best fit one's temperament and personality. Normally, this will be the prayer form that emphasizes the use of our Dominant and Auxiliary Functions. This then would be our "bread and butter" prayer, which can be used most of the time, for example, three or four days of every week. But, we should also expose ourselves, perhaps once a week, to each of the other forms of prayer. In this way we will learn to activate the transcendent dimension of all four functions. Perhaps on the weekend, when we have more time and leisure for prayer and are under less pressure from work, we could use the extra time and psychic energy to energize and use our Inferior and Tertiary Functions in prayer. If so, one may be surprised to discover that these will be the prayer times when our deepest and most beautiful experiences of God's love, power, goodness, mercy, wisdom, and presence will occur.

Just as we have Dominant and Inferior Functions, so also do we have a dominant temperament (NF, NT, SJ, SP), while its opposite is our inferior temperament. The other two basic temperaments will fall into the categories of auxiliary and tertiary temperaments. Jung always insisted that there is a polar balance between our conscious life and our unconscious. When one function or temperament is predominant in conscious activities, its opposite will be operating in unconscious areas of our life. Since many of our most intense experiences of God and grace rise out of our unconscious inner being, it behooves us not to neglect those types of prayer which require us to activate our inferior functions and inferior temperaments.

Shifts in Temperament and Methods of Prayer

The experience of many people shows that it is definitely possible for one's temperament to change in the course of life. Sometimes this is because, through education or social pressure, one has been directed into a temperament that was not in accord with one's natural or innate disposition. For some, the shift of temperament occurs deliberately when one becomes convinced of the value and need of a change of outlook or behavior in order to satisfy one's self-esteem or fulfill one's destiny. For others, the change in temperament seems to occur without any deliberate choice or even realization of what is happening until it has happened. The restlessness that occurs at the time of the mid-life crisis is often the emergence of the creative development, and better use, of our Tertiary and Inferior Functions. Jung calls these shifts of temperament "enantiodromia", a Greek word, to describe the tendency of human nature to gravitate toward its opposite at certain stages of growth toward wholeness. As we become more mature and balanced, we acquire more facility in using all the possible options for perception (S and N) and for judgment (T and F), for decisiveness (J) and flexibility (P), for extraversion (E) and introversion (I). Jung suggests that the ideal situation for a mature, whole person is that all four of the functions be situated at a mid-point between the conscious and the unconscious parts of our nature. Thus all of them will be easily available for use in our conscious activities. In *The Kingdom Within* John Sanford suggests that this was the situation of Jesus Christ, a fully mature person who was in command of all his faculties for perceiving, judging, and relating.

Different ages of history seem to have their own peculiar world-view and temperament. It appears that the present generation is pulled between the Franciscan (SP) "free spirit" temperament and spirituality and the Ignatian (SJ) conservative temperament. This thesis is somewhat corroborated by the fact that the majority of those taking part in our Prayer Project during 1982 indicated that the Franciscan type of prayer was their favorite prayer form, even though less than 10% of them tested out as belonging to the SP temperament.

However, in recent decades there has been a reaction to the over-emphasis on the "free spirit" attitude toward life. In this present generation of Americans we find a rivalry between the SP "free spirit" type of people and the SJ "law and order" people, which is evidenced in the struggle between liberals and conservatives in politics, government, religion, and even business and industry. Both present-day positions are reactions to the rational approach of the Enlightenment Period (17th-19th centuries) out of which we have emerged. The popularity of the Thomistic type of prayer during the previous centuries as contrasted with the popularity of the Franciscan, Ignatian, and Augustinian types of prayer today can be explained by this prevailing world-view or temperament of the times.

Bad experiences with a type of prayer which is unsuited to one's temperament will also build up a bias against that type of prayer. Often this prejudice is toward a distorted version of the prayer-form. Whenever one particular method of prayer is recommended as the one and only type of prayer for everyone, a negative attitude toward that kind of prayer soon arises. There is no one form of prayer that is best for every one and for every given occasion. Fanaticism with its harmful divisiveness results when we favor one method of prayer excessively and deny value to the other forms of prayer. To the adherents of one method this acceptance seems at first to bring a certain peace of mind since it does away with the tension required to maintain a balance between opposites. However, denying the value of other forms of prayer deprives us of the spiritual riches available to us when we use all four functions and all four attitudes. This, then, is why we recommend the use of all the different methods of prayer which the Christian tradition has developed during the past twenty centuries.

CHAPTER TWO

HOW TEMPERAMENT HAS AFFECTED
CHRISTIAN SPIRITUALITY

Knowing something about temperament can give us many valuable insights into the way the people of New Testament times and later generations of Christians acted and prayed. The temperament of each of the original disciples and of their successors influenced the direction they took in their relationship with God and in the teachings they passed on to us. What then were the dominant attitudes, functions, and temperaments of Jesus, the original apostles, evangelists, and saints who have greatly influenced the history of Christianity?

In *The Kingdom Within* John Sanford points out how Jesus, our Divine Lord, had the ability to use all four functions and all four attitudes in the circumstances of his life. As a fully mature person, Jesus was both Extravert and Introvert, both Sensing and Intuitive, both Thinking and Feeling, both Judging and Perceiving, depending upon the situation. The theory of temperament posits that all of us have some ability in all eight of these areas but that we tend to favor one or the other side of all four sets of preferences. Perhaps as often as 85% of the time, we will use the side we favor which is called our Dominant or Auxiliary Function rather than the opposite which is our Tertiary or Inferior function. The more mature and Christ-like we become, the more balanced we become in the use of all four attitudes and all four functions.

In the providence of God, the four men (Paul, James, John, and Peter) who were most responsible for the spirituality and growth of Christianity in the first century were of the four basic temperaments. St. Paul was of the *NF* (Intuitive-Feeling) temperament and was continually peeking around the corner to *envision* new insights about the Kingdom of God. It was through St. Paul that Christianity shed most of the oppressive shackles of Mosaic Law, for instance, the law of circumcision. St. James, the brother of the Lord, whose

21

influence on first century Christianity rivaled that of Paul, had an *SJ* (Sensing-Judging) temperament and constantly exhorted the Christians to the *duty* of implementing their faith into action in every part of their lives. St. James was the conservative, law and order man, who insisted that Christianity keep at least some of the basic Mosaic law regulations. (See Acts of the Apostles, Chapter 15:13-21.) St. John, the Beloved Disciple and the founder of the Johannine Community, was an *NT* (Intuitive-Thinking) temperament. He gave a fresh synthesis of existing *ideas* which formed Christian theology during the first century. St. John, as the contemplative, was the forerunner of the mystical tradition which in every age has been a part of the heritage of Christianity. St. Peter, the *SP* (Sensing-Perceiving) temperament, a man of *action*, had the responsibility for maintaining peace among the opposing theological schools. We see Peter using his trouble-shooting abilities during the Council of Jerusalem to reconcile Paul and James and their followers. From the point of view of the four functions, James is a Sensing Type; Paul, an Intuitive Type; John, a Thinking Type; and Peter, a Feeling Type. Peter and Paul are seen as Extraverts, while John and James are probably Introverts. Peter and Paul are primarily Perceivers (P Type persons), while John and James are Judgers (J Type persons). Therefore, the type of these four important leaders of first century Christianity would probably be: Peter—ESFP; Paul—ENFP; John—INTJ; James— ISTJ.

Similarly, due to their individual temperaments, the four evangelists (Matthew, Mark, Luke, John) give us four different viewpoints of the character, life-events, and teachings of Jesus. St. Matthew is an SJ (Sensing-Judger) temperament; St. Mark, an SP (Sensing-Perceiver); St. Luke, an NF (Intuitive-Feeler); St. John, an NT (Intuitive-Thinker). Each of them looked at the public ministry of Jesus through the eyes of their own temperament thus giving us four different insights into the richness of the personality and teachings of Jesus. Thus, St. Matthew (SJ) emphasizes continuity with the past by pointing out again and again how Jesus is the fulfillment of the prophecies of the Old Testament. Mark (SP) is very action-oriented, giving only a minimum of the the teachings of Jesus. Luke (NF) is very person-oriented and shows Jesus' great compassion for sinners, women, and outcasts. John (NT) puts a great emphasis on the importance of truth and knowledge and is the most mystical and contemplative of the four evangelists.

Just as to confine our prayer experiences to our Dominant and Auxiliary Functions or temperament would be a mistake, so too would it be a mistake to use exclusively only one Gospel in order to understand the totality of Jesus Christ and his message. Naturally, we will have our favorite Gospel, which is usually the one most closely in accord with our innate temperament; but we will miss some of the deepest experiences of the reality of God if we neglect those Gospels which we find difficult and somewhat contrary to our disposition. While it is comparatively easy to discern the basic temperament (NF, NT, SP, SJ) of the writers of the four Gospels, it is more difficult to determine to which of the sixteen types they belong since we know little about their personality other than what we can glean from the Gospels they wrote. To hazard a guess, Matthew would be an ESTJ; Mark, an ESFP; Luke, an INFP; and John, an INTJ.

Trinitarian Spirituality and Marian Devotion

During the first three centuries of Christianity the primary concern of spirituality and prayer was the development of the right attitude and relationship with the triune God and especially with Jesus Christ. Along with Trinitarianism, there sprang up a strong Marian devotion which emphasized the feminine and receptive side of prayer and spirituality. By the late third century, prayer to Mary was an important part of the Christian tradition. The earliest known prayer to Mary, the *Sub Tuum Praesidium*: "We fly to thy patronage, O holy Mother of God", goes back to this time. With a little imagination one can easily see how human temperaments and function types helped to solidify both Trinitarian spirituality and Marian devotion. The SJ temperament would be attracted especially to the Heavenly Father with His infinite goodness. The NT temperament would be attracted to Jesus Christ, the Logos, the Word of God, who is Eternal Truth. The NF temperament would be attracted to the Holy Spirit who by love invisibly unites the Church with God the Father and Jesus Christ the Risen Lord. The SP temperament would be attracted to the beauties of Mary with her creatureliness and openness to God. Trinitarian spirituality reached its zenith in the decisions of the Council of Nicea (325) and the Council of Chalcedon (451). Marian devotion reached a high water mark with the decisions of the Council of Ephesus (432) when Mary was officially defined *"Theotokos"* or Mother of God.

Looking at Trinitarian and Marian spirituality from the point of view of the four functions, devotion to God the Father highlights the Feeling Function with special emphasis upon God's goodness and mercy. Jesus Christ came on earth to proclaim this good news (Gospel) of God's loving and merciful goodness and to update the Old Testament concept of God from Lord and Creator to that of merciful Father and Provider. God the Son as the divine Logos (Word of God) speaks to the Thinking Function with the new truths and insights which Jesus' Incarnation brought to mankind. God the Holy Spirit manifested in the seven-fold gifts, especially the Gift of Wisdom, calls forth the Intuitive Function, the creativeness of which sees unity not only between Father and Son but also between God and the whole of creation. Finally, devotion to Mary elicits the Sensing Function which is used to appreciate the beauty and order of God's creation. Thus the four transcendental values of goodness, truth, unity, and beauty represent the spiritual expression of the four functions of Feeling, Thinking, Intuition, and Sensing and are in turn vitalized by devotion to the three persons of the Trinity and the Blessed Mother.

The Spirituality of the Desert Fathers and Mothers

The union of the Church and State under Constantine saw the beginnings of a new spirituality. Bloody martyrdom, or simply the constant possibility of it during the first three centuries, demanded heroic practice of the Gospel teachings. After 313 A.D., when the practice of Christianity was no longer illegal, the mass of Christians began to lead a life of adaptation to the secular world. Because of this "watering down" of the ideal Christian life, many men and women fled to the desert in order to practice asceticism, detachment, and austerity in a cenobitic life in the caves and deserts of Egypt, Palestine, and Syria. This exodus to the desert, begun in the fourth century, resulted in a new type of spirituality known as the "white" martyrdom to distinguish it from the "red" or bloody martyrdom of the previous centuries. St. Jerome and John Cassian are two well-known devout men from the West who went to the desert fathers to study and to learn this new desert spirituality.

When we study the spirituality of the desert fathers and mothers, we find that they made full use of the four psychological functions during prayer. **Sensing:** they practiced mortification of their senses in order to open their souls to the Spirit. **Thinking:** there was daily meditation upon the basic truths of faith as revealed in the Scriptures. **Feeling:** they attempted to maintain a constant, personal relationship with God the Father, Jesus the Risen Lord, and the Holy Spirit. **Intuition:** they experienced a deep, contemplative union with God. In desert spirituality, all four basic temperaments were brought into operation. The **SJ** (Ignatian) temperament occupied itself with daily Gospel meditation. The **SP** (Franciscan) temperament spent the waking period of the day and frequently much of the night in spontaneous prayer. The **NF** (Augustinian) temperament was constantly striving to attain and maintain a deep, personal relationship with God and Jesus; while the **NT** (Thomistic) temperament emphasized a deep, contemplative, mystical union with God. This appeal to all the functions and temperaments is the reason for the popularity of desert spirituality and prayer over the centuries.

Two types of prayer were developed in the West from the wisdom and experience of the desert fathers and mothers. John Cassian introduced to the convents of monks and virgins in the monastic communities of the West the continual meditation or rumination on Scripture, which became the well-known *Lectio Divina* of the Rule of St. Benedict. John Cassian also learned from Abba Isaac and the other monks in the deserts of Egypt another form of meditation which today is popularly called "Centering Prayer." This same form of prayer became popular in Greece and Russia where it was called the "Jesus Prayer." (See the Image Book, *The Way of The Pilgrim*, for a good description of how the Jesus Prayer sanctified countless persons in Greece and Russia.) The Jesus Prayer and Centering Prayer activate all four psychological functions to establish a mystical union between God and oneself. The senses (Sensing) are used in the constant repetition of the words, "Lord Jesus Christ, have mercy on me, a sinner." This constant repetition, accompanied by meditation on Jesus as Savior (Thinking Function), results in an ever deeper personal relationship with Jesus (Feeling Function). Finally, the constant repetition of these words hundreds of times each day can activate the Intuitive Function and result in mystical contemplation.

Benedictine Spirituality—Lectio Divina

First introduced into the West by John Cassian and later developed and used by St. Benedict in the rule of his monastic communities, *Lectio Divina* has, over the centuries, been closely identified with Benedictine prayer and spirituality. This ancient type of prayer has probably been used by Christians more often than any other method of prayer. This is understandable since it employs all four psychological functions and therefore is an ideal form of prayer for all the different types and temperaments of personality. Four other traditional forms of Christian spirituality and prayer — Augustinian, Franciscan, Thomistic, and Ignatian — are actually variations of this most ancient of all Christian forms of prayer. The *Devotio Moderna* of the late Middle Ages also includes all four steps of *Lectio Divina*. In Chapter Three we explain more fully the four steps of *Lectio Divina* and how they make use of all four functions of Sensing, Thinking, Feeling, and Intuition. We will also suggest some examples of how one might use *Lectio Divina* in a daily period of prayer.

Augustinian Spirituality and Prayer

Throughout the Christian era, the Church Fathers and spiritual masters have insisted that the words of the Bible can be transposed to relate to the needs of every individual and every generation. The inspired writers of the Bible were able to penetrate the eternal wisdom of God and applied their insights to the situations of their time; yet the infinite wisdom of God is applicable to all times and all situations of mankind. Without exception, the Fathers and Doctors of the Church have practiced transposition of the Words of God as part of their daily prayer and taught their disciples to use this same method to discern the path God willed for them. We call this method Augustinian Prayer. St. Augustine was not the only one who taught personal reflection on the presence of God in His Word. However, the Rule of Life which St. Augustine developed for the communities established by him became the basic method of spirituality followed by many religious communities in succeeding centuries. Thus we honor him by naming this type of prayer Augustinian.

Augustinian prayer uses all four functions but special emphasis is placed upon the use of Intuition and Feeling, making it especially adaptable to the NF temperament. St. Augustine as well as a great many canonized saints, spiritual masters, and seekers of The Way, are more than likely to be of the NF temperament. Of the four basic temperaments this temperament has the greatest drive for self-development and spiritual growth. This has been amply proved in the Prayer Project where 48% of those participating were NFs and is evidenced in the retreat movement where NFs are almost always in the majority. In Chapter Five we will explain more fully the Augustinan method of prayer and give some examples for your use.

Franciscan Spirituality and Prayer

At the beginning of the thirteenth century, St. Francis of Assisi revolutionized the Church and the medieval world by introducing a new type of spirituality, which attracted not only large numbers of the ordinary lay people but also clergy and religous and won the approval of the Popes and the Roman Curia. St. Francis probably understood the Gospel teaching of Jesus as well as, or better than, any Christian of any age. Once he was converted to the Lord, he resolved to follow the Gospel as literally and totally as possible. The result was a way of prayer and spirituality totally open to the guidance of the Holy Spirit and with a simplicity and directness that could be understood easily even by the uneducated.

Franciscan spirituality and prayer has had many followers in every century and seems to have a special appeal today. In the responses to our prayer questionaires during the Prayer Project, there was a strong preference for the Franciscan type of prayer by all personality types. This is understandable since we are living in a period that has a free-spirited and open attitude. Many of us today are Franciscans at heart and are charmed with the spirit of abandon, humor, and magnetism revealed in the human interest anecdotes we have heard and read about St. Francis. However, there is more to Franciscan spirituality than the poetry of a free spirit who rejoices in the beauties and glories of God in nature.

St. Francis is called *Il Poverello*, the little poor man, because he made a deliberate decision to give away all his worldly possessions and depend solely upon the charity of others for everything, even the bread he ate. How many of us are willing to adopt this aspect of Franciscan spirituality? With all of our concern about security, insurance, pension plans, etc., can we honestly say that we are willing to undertake the Franciscan way of blind, total trust in God? We are probably so far removed from the poverty of St. Francis that for us even to imagine how it might be put into practice today is almost impossible. The modern attraction to St. Francis is one more way that divine grace is calling us to divest ourselves of our excessive attachment to worldly goods and material prosperity and follow the way of the *Il Poverello*.

St. Ignatius of Loyola states that the third and highest degree of humility is the desire to be like Jesus Christ to the extent of desiring to suffer the same afflictions, the same rejection and persecution, the same hatred and torture as Jesus did. St. Francis so desired union with the sufferings of Jesus that before he died he experienced the Stigmata, the same wounds that Jesus suffered on the cross. These open wounds shed blood and severely pained Francis during the last years of his life. An additional humiliation occurred when the brothers of his own community turned against him and rejected him as their leader in favor of Brother Elias. This third and highest degree of humility is beautifully illustrated in the story of how St. Francis taught Brother Leo that perfect joy is to be found not in heroic deeds but in bearing the Cross. (See *Little Flowers of St. Francis*, Part I, #8.)

The basic temperament of St. Francis was SP (Sensing-Perceiving); and we have called the type of prayer and spirituality which especially appeals to the SP temperament Franciscan prayer and spirituality. In Chapter Six we will explain this type of prayer and give some Franciscan prayer exercises for one to use.

Thomistic Spirituality and Prayer

At the same time that Francis of Assisi was developing his spirituality in Italy, another type of spirituality was being developed in Spain and France by St. Dominic. Dominican spirituality developed in the large medieval universities of Paris, Bologna, and elsewhere and had special appeal to the intellectuals of the day in their search of truth. The most famous son of St. Dominic was St. Thomas Aquinas who lived a generation after St. Dominic's death. Because of the tremendous influence of the theology of St. Thomas on the spirituality of so many Christians, instead of calling this spirituality and prayer Dominican, we have called it Thomistic.

Thomistic prayer appeals especially to the NT temperament with its interest and search for truth and competency. It has been popular among the intellectual leaders of Roman Catholicism and also among Protestant leaders of the Enlightenment down through the centuries until the present era. However, unless they happened to be of the NT temperament, the common people found this type of prayer especially difficult. Yet, this method was most often recommended in the books on prayer during the Enlightenment and throughout the Tridentine Period of Catholicity, right up to the Second Vatican Council. Because the impression was given that this type of prayer was the best method of prayer for everyone and should be used by all, many, including priests and nuns trained in seminaries and convents, found prayer difficult, or even impossible, and often abandoned its practice. In Chapter Seven we explain Thomistic prayer more fully and give some practical ways to use it.

Devotio Moderna

During the fourteenth and fifteenth centuries there was a

reaction against the over-emphasis by the Scholastics on intellectuality and excessive use of the Thinking Function. In the low countries of Holland and Belgium a new form of prayer — *Devotio Moderna* — developed. The great emphasis was upon the use of the Feeling Function in prayer. Gerard Groote and Thomas à Kempis are the two best known advocates of this new form of prayer and spirituality. From this period comes the book, *The Imitation of Christ*, which was originally written by Groote but revised and more popularly attributed to Thomas à Kempis. These words taken from *The Imitation of Christ*: "I would rather feel contrition than know how to define it," clearly express the anti-intellectual attitude of this spirituality.

Emphasis on feeling in prayer has continued and is evidenced in the French spirituality of the eighteenth and nineteenth centuries. St. Therese of Lisieux is a modern example of the *Devotio Moderna* spirituality. Even as a young teen-ager, St. Therese had memorized all of the book, *The Imitation of Christ*, and could quote it chapter by chapter. The modern version of the *Devotio Moderna* was somewhat sugary and distasteful to many; but in recent years people are once more appreciating its value and depth.

Ignatian Spirituality and Prayer

Following the pattern of the thirteenth century when two well-known forms of spirituality developed under the guidance of St. Francis and St. Dominic, in the sixteenth century two well-known Spanish saints developed two types of spirituality. One of them was St. Ignatius of Loyola, founder of the Jesuit Order; the other, St. Teresa of Avila who reformed the Carmelite Order.

Shortly after his conversion, St. Ignatius went alone into a cave at Manresa and in the course of thirty days had an experience of prayer that profoundly influenced the rest of his life. He later developed this type of prayer into what is known as *The Spiritual Exercises of St. Ignatius*. The meditational process of the *Exercises* is more easily understood by the SJ temperament, but the NT and NF temperament also find this method of praying quite profitable. However, the SP temperament frequently has difficulty with this method of prayer. Most souls who are willing to endure the discipline of the thirty days of intense prayer activity of *The Ignatian Spiritual Exercises* are rewarded with an unforgetable spiritual experience that frequently changes the whole direction of their life. Somewhat resembling Augustinian prayer, Ignatian Prayer differs in that it *projects* the person as a participant into the different scenes and experiences of the life of Jesus and history of salvation; whereas Augustinian Prayer *transposes* the words of the Bible to our situation today. The spirituality of the liturgical year where we commemorate the events of salvation history, especially the events in the life of Jesus, is a good example of Ignatian spirituality. This type of prayer is explained more fully in Chapter Four and suggestions for its use are given.

Teresian Spirituality

St. Teresa of Avila treats many different forms of prayer in her writings, but she is most famous for her discussion of prayer for those who have reached the higher levels of passive contemplation. In the terminology of St. Teresa these would be the types of prayer appropriate to those who have reached the fourth, fifth, sixth, and seventh spiritual mansions. (See her book *Interior Castle*.) Just as the Benedictine *Lectio Divina* is appropriate for all types and temperaments so are St. Teresa's recommendations for contemplation suitable for all types of human personality. St. John of the Cross with his discussion of the "dark nights" which are frequently endured by contemplatives gives another dimension of Teresian prayer and spirituality. In this book we do not give a full explanation of Teresian contemplation since it does not seem to depend upon temperament but stands in a class by itself and is open to all temperaments and personalities.

CHAPTER THREE

BENEDICTINE PRAYER — LECTIO DIVINA

Lectio Divina is a type of prayer suitable to all four basic temperaments: SJ, SP, NF, and NT. It also employs to full advantage all of the four psychological functions: Sensing, Intuition, Thinking, and Feeling. Both Judging Types and Perceiving Types like this method since it can be either as structured or as flexible as one chooses. Furthermore, *Lectio Divina* can be used by Extraverts in relating to the outer world or by Introverts in relating to the inner world of the spirit. Therefore, it is no surprise that it is both one of the oldest and most popular of all forms of prayer in the Christian tradition.

Lectio Divina is a method of prayer that goes back to the fourth and fifth centuries. Easily and quickly translated as "sacred reading," it can be that only; but using sacred reading as the base, it becomes a ladder of escalation or intensification of prayer with four steps: reading, meditation, prayer, and contemplation. Traditionally we use the four Latin equivalents to express these four steps: **Lectio, Meditatio, Oratio, Contemplatio**.

In all likelihood the monastic practice of *Lectio Divina* was brought to the West from the Eastern desert fathers by John Cassian at the beginning of the fifth century. However, it has been closely connected to St. Benedict and Benedictine spirituality since its development and popularity began in the communities of monks and virgins founded by St. Benedict. Furthermore, this method of prayer is highly recommended even today by Benedictines and Cistercians. Many later forms of prayer developed by Christians are based upon this prayer method. As different versions of *Lectio Divina*, they use and emphasize the four psychological functions: Sensing, Intuition, Thinking, and Feeling. Therefore we find this form of prayer is appropriate for all four of the basic temperaments and all sixteen individual types of human personality.

Corresponding to the four basic psychological functions, there

31

are four steps to *Lectio Divina* which call forth the use of each of these functions. (1) **Lectio** uses the **Senses** either in spiritual reading or in perceiving the works of the Lord. (2) **Meditatio** uses the psychological function of **Thinking** (the intellect) to reflect upon the insights presented in **Lectio**. (3) **Oratio** calls forth one's **Feeling** Function to personalize the new insights so that one may enter into a personal dialogue or communication with God. (4) Finally, in **Contemplatio** one's **Intuition** is used in order to coalesce the experience of the previous three steps. In this time of quiet one is open to the inspirations of the Holy Spirit which may come by way of new insights, new perceptions, or a new infusion of peace, joy, and love which is part of the mystical union of which the saints tell us.

In the twelfth century the Carthusian Prior Guigo II describes *Lectio Divina* as follows in *The Monastic Ladder or Treatise on a Method of Prayer* (Section X): "Reading, you should seek; meditating, you will find; praying, you shall call; and contemplating, the door will be opened to you." And, then, there is the contemporary description of *Lectio Divina* by a Southern rural minister who, when asked how he prayed, replied: "I reads myself full; I thinks myself clear; I prays myself hot; I lets myself cool."

The four steps of *Lectio Divina* respond to the characteristics of all four of the basic temperaments. **Lectio** or spiritual reading appeals especially to the SJ temperament within each of us. Through it we study and search the Scriptures and other religious writings to discover within this wisdom of the ages the direction and guidance for our daily life. **Meditatio** or reflection upon these ideas and insights culled from the spiritual reading gives answers to the NT (seeking) temperament. In this portion of *Lectio Divina* we try to personalize the message received in **Lectio** either by transposition or projection. In transposition (the Augustinian method) we try to imagine these words being spoken directly to us, i.e., as if God or Jesus is speaking them to us personally. In projection (the Ignatian method) we put ourselves back into the biblical situation and try to imagine that we are present as the words or events first occurred and then try to draw some practical fruit from this experience.

The third part of *Lectio Divina*, **Oratio**, appeals both to the NF and the SP temperaments. In this step we dialogue with the Lord and respond personally to what He has said to us. Thus we enter into an intimate relationship with God, Jesus, and the Holy Spirit. Feelings of love, joy, gratitude, sorrow, repentance, desire, enthusiasm, conviction, commitment are activated and verbalized in spontaneous prayers of love, thanksgiving, sorrow, dedication, and petition.

The fourth portion, **Contemplatio**, is a time just to be quiet, to listen, and to be open to whatever the Lord might wish to impart. The creatively perceptive NF temperament sees this fourth step as an introduction to the contemplative type of prayer of which all of us are capable. We can expect some distractions at this time, but they should not disturb us. When one becomes aware of distractions, one simply recalls the theme of the **Lectio** and tries once again to be open and attentive to whatever new perceptions, insights, inspirations, thoughts, or practical applications that appear. This fourth part might be thought of as "resting in the Lord" . . . just being present to the enjoyment of being alone with Him. This is a time for the activation of our intuitive faculties in order to catch any reconciling symbols that might emerge from the depths of our unconscious.

Lectio Divina is a method of prayer that is suitable for both the beginner and the spiritually advanced. Its progress from hearing the Word of God to studying it, reflecting upon it, praying upon it, and adapting it to our situation leads one deeper and deeper into the longed-for union with God. By considering each step on this ladder of prayer, we can see how we may be helped on our spiritual journey.

Lectio

Lectio is the eager seeking after the Word of God and divine truth and the way by which God's truth is imparted to us. The revelation of God's truth is found primarily in the Sacred Scriptures; but God also reveals His Presence in other books, in created nature, in other people, in the events of history, and in the events of divine providence. God usually reveals His truth through the works of other human beings who have discovered and shared it through their writings, their lives, their works of art, and other forms of expression. The authors of the books of the Bible were inspired by the Holy Spirit, so we believe the Holy Spirit is the primary author of these books. But God also inspires others and speaks to us through the words and works of all his creatures.

Meditatio

As long as the Word of God is in a book, or in nature, or in the word and work of someone else, it will not have the effect upon us that God intends it to have. Therefore through **Meditatio** we must welcome the Word of God into our lives and turn it from a dead word into the living word and presence of God. Having received God's truth, we need to chew it and ruminate upon it as a cow does upon its cud. Through meditation we discover the beauty and goodness of God's truth and apply it to our own situation and needs. Thus we bring to life the meaning of divine revelation as we personalize and adapt it to our daily living.

Oratio

Our response to this revealed truth is the **Oratio**. We can accept the Word of God or dismiss its value for us. We are free to reflect and meditate upon it and try to relate its meaning to our life; or we can reject it as of no worth or no value to us. In the **Oratio** we decide what changes we want to make in our life as a result of the truth of God that has been revealed to us. At this time we decide whether we will incorporate the Word of God into our heart, our life, and our work or whether we will rationalize a rejection of its efficacy for us. Our response is expressed through words, thoughts, desires, feelings, resolutions, decisions, commitments, dedications; or through sorrow for past failures; through gratitude, praise, petition.

In this third step of *Lectio Divina* we use the four different kinds of prayer described in the old Baltimore Catechism: Adoration, Contrition, Thanksgiving, and Supplication. As an aid to perk our memory the acronym, ACTS, was coined. It is important to note that these four types of prayer (adoration, contrition, thanksgiving, and supplication or petition) belong to the third step of *Lectio Divina*. All of them are part of our personal response to God's Word. To limit our prayer merely to these four responses to God's Word would be a grave error. Prayer is a dialogue in which we both listen to God and then respond to Him. All too often we limit prayer to a monologue of our speaking to God, and even limit that primarily to petition or supplication. True prayer is, first and foremost, listening to God speaking to us and then, secondarily, responding to God's words to us.

Contemplatio

In **Contemplatio** we seek to effect the union of love that should result from our dialogue with God. This is meant to be the consummation of the union of our mind and God's truth, of our heart and God's love, of our life and God's life, of our person and the person of God. This consummation can be neither hurried nor forced. We need to give ample time and undistracted attention to the word, truth, or task at hand if we hope to experience any kind of mystical union with God here on earth. Frequently, we will go through the whole exercise of *Lectio Divina* without being aware of this union with God occurring. If so, it is quite possible that through either some fault of our own or circumstances beyond our control (i.e., outside interruptions and distractions) we were not properly disposed for this union with God. On the other hand, this action can be so quiet, so deep, and so spiritual that we are not consciously aware of it happening, but there is a way to know if it has occurred. Our Lord says: "By your fruits you will know them" (Matt 7:16) and St. Paul tells us the fruits of the Holy Spirit are: "love, joy, peace, patience, generosity, faithfulness, kindness, gentleness, self-control, purity" (Gal 5:22-23). If we become aware later that there has been an increase in any one of these attributes within us, we can be assured that our *Lectio Divina* has been successful and God has truly touched and reached us.

Aids for the Use of Lectio Divina

There are certain things we can do to make the prayer period in which we use *Lectio Divina* more rewarding and uplifting. First, we should choose the time of the day when we are most alert, least distracted, least tired, most well-rested, and without outside pressure. In other words, we should set aside prime time each day for prayer. Secondly, we should seek a place that is quiet and restful, warm or cool as needed, comfortable, and conducive to giving our full attention to God and God's Word.

Having found the best possible time and place for one's prayer, one should select a passage of Sacred Scripture, or some other spiritual reading, appropriate to one's present needs. There are many ways to make a choice of the proper text. One may follow a recommended list of texts or topics from some book or leaflet. One may simply take a whole book of the Bible, like one of the Gospels, and read it through slowly, chapter by chapter, while consulting a good commentary on the text. If possible, this process of hunting and fishing to discover the text, or word, or idea that speaks to us and is appropriate for prayer and reflection should be done beforehand, perhaps the previous night. Then we will be ready to use this text on the following day for our period of *Lectio Divina* .

The next day at the selected time we should read the chosen text again slowly several times, trying to savor each word and phrase, making sure that we come to a good understanding of what the text is saying. It sometimes helps to read the text aloud. Then **Meditatio** or reflection upon the text follows, as we try to personalize it so that it speaks to our particular needs. It is helpful to have a notebook or pad of paper handy to note insights and reflections. Our notes should be read over several times and reflected upon, and new insights should be added as they occur. From time to time, we should go back to the text originally selected and reread it to discover if some innuendo or insight was missed. Then record this finding in the notebook and again reread the material in the notebook.

The third step, **Oratio**, is our response to the Word of God. This can easily be intermingled with the **Meditatio**, so that together these two become a dialogue between God and ourselves. God speaks to us; and we respond with gratitude, love, petition, contrition, praise, sorrow, joy, commitment, dedication. Listening and responding to God can go on for a long time; and the dialogue can become intensely personal, intimate, and full of emotion. A heartfelt reaction of some kind should occur if the prayer is to have lasting results and bring about a change in our life. The feelings may be deep but without visible manifestation, such as tears; but we should be seriously committed to whatever we say to God in response to His Word. Of course there will be days when we are so tired or distracted that our feelings are not aroused; but, if we have the right intention and make the effort, God will be satisfied; and the time spent will not be wasted.

In the final step, **Contemplatio**, we must give God ample opportunity to reveal Himself anew to us. God must never be hurried. He sets the pace and keeps His own time schedule. Therefore, we must be willing to wait upon the Lord. We do not tell Him what, or when, or how, but let Him tell us. This requires silence, stillness, and a willingness to wait until the Lord Himself moves our heart, stirs up our will, and enlightens our mind. "Be still and know that I am God" (Psalm 46:11). Having prepared ourselves by reading, meditation, and prayer, we now await and hope for whatever graces God might see fit to send our way. Many times we will not be aware of anything happening, but we should trust that the grace of God is working within the depths of our soul. God asks blind faith and trust of us.

The four steps of *Lectio Divina* may be followed in any order we choose so that one may go from one to the other and then back again. For example, quiet periods for contemplation can be interspersed throughout the reading, meditation, and oration. Meditation and oration can be used interchangeably, going from one to the other and then back again. Also, one should return frequently to rereading the text in order to discern any new insights. Complete freedom should be followed in the order and variety of the four steps during the prayer period. One must try to be completely open to the guidance and inspirations of the Holy Spirit. This means going with our thoughts in whatever direction that seems right and best at the time. We should never hesitate to experiment and try new ways so that we may discover the method best suited to our needs at the time.

A spiritual journal is frequently a great help to people when using *Lectio Divina*. This journal may be an ordinary notebook in which we write all or part of any exchanges between God and ourselves that occur during the time set aside for prayer. In it we note any insights that come to us during our reading, meditation, and contemplation. We also enter in it our responses during the **Oratio** or other times during the prayer period. Such a written record of our dialogue with God is a wonderful way of imprinting our prayer experiences upon our memory so that we can more easily recall them later when needed.

FIFTEEN PRAYER SUGGESTIONS FOR USING *LECTIO DIVINA*

These suggestions are based upon the Sunday selections from St. Matthew's Gospel, Cycle A, tenth to twenty-fourth Sundays of Ordinary Time. It is suggested that at least one commentary be used in connection with the prayer period. A recommended commentary is *Matthew* by John P. Meier (Michael Glazier, Inc., Wilmington, Delaware 19801).

PRAYER SUGGESTION #1:
LECTIO: Read Matthew 9:9-13 and Meier, pp. 92-95.
MEDITATIO: Jesus came to call sinners, the unworthy. God is merciful. Therefore, none of us need ever be discouraged or imagine that we are unworthy of being in the presence of God and Christ. However, having received God's gracious invitation and assurance of mercy and forgiveness, we now have the duty to follow Jesus in his example of mercy and forgiveness toward those who have offended us. This also means following Jesus in a life of victimhood, The Way of The Cross.
ORATIO: Respond to the call of Jesus by inviting him to join in a fellowship conversation. Dialogue with him, tell him our joy at his Good News and our gratitude for God's mercy and forgiveness. Resolve to be ready to forgive others and to be united with those who have offended us. This is the time to make known to ourselves and to the Lord our resolutions of how we intend to follow Jesus in The Way of the Cross and victimhood.
CONTEMPLATIO: Be still and be open to any insights, thoughts, desires, resolutions, peace, joy, or love that come to our attention.

PRAYER SUGGESTION #2:
LECTIO: Read Matthew 9:36 to 10:8 and Meier, pp. 100-107.
MEDITATIO: The compassion of Jesus for the people of his time is the model for our own compassion for the people of our time who are wandering aimlessly, not knowing where to go. Not only should we pray for vocations to Christian ministry, but we ourselves should also respond to the call to ministry. Having been summoned

to ministry by Jesus, we are given the power and authority to expel unclean spirits, cure sickness and disease, which would include spiritual diseases. All of this should be done freely without asking anything in return except what is necessary to sustain one's life and ministry. "Freely you have received, freely you should give."

ORATIO   Respond personally to the call of Jesus to ministry. Pray not only for the call of others but that you too will respond generously to God's call.

CONTEMPLATIO: Be open to any thought, desires, insights concerning how one might do more in ministering to others.

PRAYER SUGGESTION #3:

LECTIO: Read Matthew 10:26-33 and Meier, pp. 111-112.

MEDITATIO: What are my present fears in regard to my ministry? What is it, or who is it, that presently intimidates me? Where have I failed to minister because of fear? What does this Gospel passage say in regard to overcoming these fears? The only one we need to fear is God, yet Jesus assures us that we are worth more to God than all of the created world. The only time we need to fear is when we are ashamed of our relationship to Christ and disown it before the people of this world. Where and when have I hidden my Christianity and remained silent?

ORATIO: Beg God for the courage to profess one's faith regardless of the situation or person and ask His forgiveness for this fear which shows a lack of faith.

CONTEMPLATIO: Maintain silence in order to catch any new insights.

PRAYER SUGGESTION #4:

LECTIO: Read Matthew 10:37-42 and Meier, pp. 112-115.

MEDITATIO: Where have I sought only myself in my work, in my family, in my recreation, in my leisure time, in my Church work? Can I think of some instances in my life where the seeking of self has brought ruin upon whatever I was doing? Can I think of an instance where I have sacrificed myself for the sake of God or others? What happened as a result?

ORATIO: Pray for the grace to put oneself last and God and others first.

CONTEMPLATIO: Be open to any insights about the value of self-sacrifice.

PRAYER SUGGESTION #5:

LECTIO: Read Matthew 11:25-30 and Meier, pp. 126-128.

MEDITATIO: Jesus gives us an example from his own life of how we should pray. How much is this like our own way of praying? Do gratitude and praise of God predominate our thoughts? Do we show the same gracious acceptance of God's will in our regard? What can we change in our present life to allow Jesus to reveal himself and the Father to us? How do we respond to the gentle, loving invitation of Jesus to come to him when we are heavily laden? Jesus says, "Learn from me for I am gentle, meek, humble, and lowly of heart." What would this involve in our life? What changes would be needed? Jesus assures us that his yoke is easy and his burden light. Have we found this to be true? What does carrying the yoke of service for Christ involve?

ORATIO: There is much food for personal response to Jesus in this passage. Try to activate feelings of love, joy, generosity, contrition, dedication. Try to pray to the Heavenly Father in the same way that Jesus does in this passage.

CONTEMPLATIO: Read these words of Jesus over several times and then just be quiet and allow their meaning to sink deeply into your mind, conscience, heart, and soul.

PRAYER SUGGESTION #6:

LECTIO: Read Matthew 13:1-23 and Meier, pp. 141-146.

MEDITATIO: Jesus gives six different results of his sowing of the seed. Three of them do not produce any fruit, but three of them do: 30, 60, 100 fold. Think of the different times in your life where these six situations have occurred. There have been times when we have heard the Word of God, say at Sunday liturgy, but before we get home, we have totally forgotten it (the first situation!). There have been times when we have heard the Word with great enthusiasm; but a week later it has withered away (second group!). Think of the times when we have heard God's word, applied it to our situation, and have done something in response to it for a while, but then the cares and concerns of this world have choked out our good resolutions so that no good fruit resulted. Think also of the times when God's Word did produce good and abundant fruit in our life — perhaps even a hundred fold.

ORATIO: Having applied the parable to our own life, respond accordingly. There probably will be room for contrition, regret for past failures, fervent prayers for help in the present, good resolutions for the future. What can you say to God to insure that you will be in one of the groups who produce good fruit rather than in one of those who fail to produce any fruit?

CONTEMPLATIO: What new insights is the Holy Spirit giving you from reflecting on this parable of the sower and the seed?

PRAYER SUGGESTION #7:

LECTIO: Read Matthew 13:24-43 and Meier, pp. 147-151.

MEDITATIO: This parable of the cockle and the wheat can be applied either to our need of tolerance and patience with others in our community who seem to represent the cockle or to the mixture of good and bad in our own life. Where have we been too energetic in our attempts to root up the cockle in our community before the time of harvest? How should we show more patience with our own faults, the weeds or cockle within our character? The dividing line between good and evil (wheat and cockle) runs through the middle of our heart as well as through the middle of the hearts of other individuals and communities. There is a right time to root out the faults that have been allowed to grow up beside the virtues. It would be harmful if we tried to eradicate them too quickly. What then are the particular faults that at present we should be trying to root up and remove from our soul.

ORATIO: We should pray fervently for light and guidance from the Holy Spirit to discern the cockle (faults) in our life. Pray also that the little mustard seed, or leaven of God's grace, will not be allowed to die out or be wasted. With patience we can hope that it will grow until our whole life is shot through with God.

CONTEMPLATIO: Be perfectly quiet and try to discern God's time schedule in regard to conquering the various faults of our personality. At what does the Lord wish us to work at this time?

PRAYER SUGGESTION #8:

LECTIO: Read Matthew 13:44-52 and Meier, pp. 151-154.

MEDITATIO: What is the hidden treasure and the pearl of great price which is awaiting our discovery? "The reign of God (or the kingdom of God) is like a hidden treasure or pearl of great price." Have we discovered the reign (the kingdom) of God in our life? What does this mean? It is that situation where God and God's will become the center of our whole life, our every thought, word, deed, decision, desire. Once we have discovered this, we should be ready to sacrifice everything to obtain it. Is this true in my life? The kingdom of God is the situation where God has total freedom to do whatever he pleases with us and with the world. We are able to use our freedom to thwart God's will for us and thus hinder or hold back the establishment of the kingdom of God.

ORATIO: With as much feeling as possible, beg God for the grace to discover, recognize, and appreciate the value of the kingdom of God in one's life. Having discovered its meaning, one can devote one's whole energy to attaining it and pay whatever the price needed to obtain it. Beg God for the grace to sacrifice everything else if necessary.

CONTEMPLATIO: Be open to uncovering the particular meaning of the kingdom of God for you in your life. Be open to the price to be paid in order to obtain it.

PRAYER SUGGESTION #9:

LECTIO: Read Matthew 14:13-21 and Meier, pp. 161-163.

MEDITATIO: Jesus has compassion on the multitude. Today, a multitude of the world's people are hungry and dying of famine. What can we do to relieve this poverty and destitution? God continues to perform on earth the multiplication of the loaves and fishes; for there is more than enough land and opportunity to feed all. The problem is one of distribution. Just as in the Gospel story Jesus depended upon his disciples to distribute the loaves and fishes, we too, his disciples, have a responsibility to bring about a more equitable distribution of the riches of the world today. What am I doing about this? What can I do?

ORATIO: Pray for the grace and courage to do something about the world's hunger.

CONTEMPLATIO: Be open to any inspirations that God may wish to give.

PRAYER SUGGESTION #10:

LECTIO: Read Matthew 14:22-33 and Meier, pp. 163-166.

MEDITATIO: Jesus comes walking on the water to save us whenever we are in trouble and when the winds of adversity are against us. His appearance startles us at times, but he reassures us, "Get hold of yourselves. It is I, do not be afraid." Once Jesus joins us in our boat, the winds of adversity quickly die down. We too can walk on water. Think of the different times we have had an experience similar to that of Peter.

ORATIO: When have we failed to recognize Jesus' approach when we were in danger? Where have we acted like Peter and faltered in our faith? What can we do to assure our recognition of Him in time of trouble? How can we build up our courage and trust?

CONTEMPLATIO: Be still and accept a deeper faith and trust in God.

PRAYER SUGGESTION #11:
LECTIO: Read Matthew 15:21-28 and Meier, pp. 171-173.
MEDITATIO: Jesus finds it impossible to resist the faith and persistence of the Canaanite woman. If we are persistent in our petitions and ask with faith, we too will be irresistible when we pray to the Lord. Where are we lacking in our faith when we go to God in prayer? What within us needs healing at present? What demon that oppresses us do we need to ask the Lord to remove?
ORATIO: During this part of our prayer period, let us try to follow the example of the woman in the Gospel when we make our requests. Make sure that what we ask for is in accord with God's will; otherwise always ask on the condition that it be in accord with His will. "Not my will, but your will, O God, be done." Show the same humility as this woman and reflect upon our own lowliness; but like her, do not take "no" for an answer. Be persistent but humble in petitioning.
CONTEMPLATIO: Be open to any changes in our way of praying that God might be asking.

PRAYER SUGGESTION #12:
LECTIO: Read Matthew 16:13-20 and Meier, pp. 178-183.
MEDITATIO: "Who do you say that I am?" What does Jesus mean to me? How often do I think of him in the course of an ordinary day? Is he truly the center of my life? What more can I do to make him the center of my every thought, desire, word, deed? In what way can we say that the church community in which we live is also built upon the rock of our faith? What can I do to increase my faith in Jesus Christ?
ORATIO: Pray to Jesus for the faith of Peter. Pray that all whose faith is dependent upon you will be strengthened in their faith in Jesus Christ and their faith not be weakened or lost because of something you may do or fail to do.
CONTEMPLATIO: Seek any new insights that might come concerning Jesus Christ.

PRAYER SUGGESTION #13:
LECTIO: Read Matthew 16:21-27 and Meier, pp. 183-188.
MEDITATIO: What does "to deny myself and take up my cross and follow in the footsteps of Jesus" mean in my life? What are the crosses in my present life? How in today's world can I be a victim of love after the example of Jesus? How is God asking me to lose my life for His sake? Do I deserve the same rebuke as Peter for

my attitude toward suffering and sacrifice? How do I make the same mistake as Peter in judging by the standards of this world rather than by the standards of God?

ORATIO: Try to put yourself in the place of Peter and imagine how he must have felt to be so severely rebuked by Jesus. Enter with as much feeling as possible into Jesus' struggle to accept the cross that the Heavenly Father willed for him to carry. Be open to the full trauma of Jesus' teaching about the necessity to deny ourselves and take up our cross and follow him on the road to Calvary. Pray for the grace to accept whatever crosses God's providence sees fit to allow to come into our life.

CONTEMPLATIO: Be open to the insights about suffering and self-denial which the Lord may impart at this time.

PRAYER SUGGESTION #14:

LECTIO: Read Matthew 18:15-20 and Meier, pp. 204-206.

MEDITATIO: In this passage Jesus teaches us one of the most difficult of all the works of mercy: admonishing the sinner. Very few people are able to do a good job of this act of charity — namely, helping others to recognize their faults and do something about changing their lives. Think of the times in one's own life where one has criticized another for some fault but did more harm than good. Can you think of some time when fraternal correction was successful? What can you do to be more successful in carrying out this particular work of mercy? Is there anyone you should attempt to admonish — for example, someone who drinks too much or indulges in some other excess? Jesus says we should first attempt the fraternal correction alone; and then, if necessary, take another when we attempt the intervention; finally, if the situation is serious enough, bring it to the attention of the whole community.

ORATIO: Having considered a situation where one might practice fraternal correction, pray fervently for the light to know how best to handle it and for the courage to do it.

CONTEMPLATIO: Be open to the guidance of the Holy Spirit.

PRAYER SUGGESTION #15:

LECTIO: Read Matthew 18:21-35 and Meier, pp. 207-209.

MEDITATIO: Jesus says that we must be willing to forgive seventy times seven. This can apply to the something which may have occurred many years ago but caused such a deep hurt that even though we have previously forgiven the person we need to reinstitute the process of forgiveness again and again. Unless we willingly forgive our neighbor, God will not forgive us our faults. Is there anyone who has hurt me in the past that I have not yet forgiven completely? What do I do about it now?

ORATIO: Pray the Lord's Prayer, especially the second part, and try to mean it as deeply and sincerely as possible. Pray for each person who has in some way hurt or offended you in the past. This is the first step to forgiveness.

CONTEMPLATIO: Be open to the possibility that one needs to forgive again and again.

CHAPTER FOUR

IGNATIAN PRAYER AND SPIRITUALITY
THE SJ TEMPERAMENT

The method of prayer which we call Ignatian Prayer is a way of prayer even more ancient than the *Lectio Divina* which was developed in the fourth century. This way of praying was used by the Israelites a thousand to twelve hundred years before the birth of Christ. Its basic trait is the remembrance of an event of salvation history. This commemoration, however, is more than a pious recalling of an event which occurred many years previously; for by immersion in its recollection the praying people relive, participate in, and in a symbolic way make real the past events. All four functions are involved and the same structure is followed as in *Lectio Divina*.

Among Christians, St. Ignatius of Loyola, the founder of the Jesuit Order, was the great teacher of this way of praying. Hence, we have called this type of prayer and spirituality Ignatian in his honor. The *Spiritual Exercises*, which were written by Ignatius after an intense spiritual experience in a cave in Manresa, where he had retired to pray, give us an outline to follow and commemorate the life of Our Lord Jesus Christ. Those employing the Ignatian method of prayer strive to participate in the actual event by projecting themselves back into the historical happening to try to become a part of the scene in order to draw some practical fruit for their life. The sensible imagination is employed so that by reliving the event in an affective manner one can come to real sorrow, joy, or resolution of amendment. For example, St. Ignatius in the contemplation on the Nativity of Jesus in the *Spiritual Exercises* suggests: "I will make myself a poor, little, unworthy servant, and as though present, look upon them, contemplate them, and serve them in their needs with all possible homage and reverence. Then I will reflect on myself that I may reap some fruit."

The Ignatian style of prayer can be utilized by all temperaments, although people of the SP and NT temperament may have some difficulty with this type of prayer. However, Ignatian Prayer best suits the SJ temperament (which is called the Epimethean temperament in *Please Understand Me* by David Kiersey). Approximately 40% of the general population are of the SJ temperament; and probably 50% or more of those who regularly attend church on Sunday are also of this temperament. From our observations in parishes during retreats and workshops, more than half of those in attendance at any church group meeting are apt to be of the SJ temperament. The SJ person has a very strong sense of duty and obligation, whether it be to God or to fellow human beings. Therefore, SJs are usually the people who continue going to church even though religion may lose its appeal for the other three temperaments.

The early development of the Christian Liturgical Year with its yearly commemorations of the events in the life of Jesus is a sign of the influence of SJ persons in the early Church; and the fact that Ignatian Prayer has been so popular down through the centuries may be explained by the preponderance of SJs among church-going persons. The best example of Ignatian Prayer in today's liturgy is the Liturgy of Holy Week. Beginning on Palm Sunday and carrying through to Easter Sunday, we commemorate in vivid detail each part of the Passion, Death, and Resurrection of Jesus. Those who participate in the Holy Week Services are taken back two thousand years and become a part of each event. From this participation some practical fruit for their present relationship with God and neighbor is drawn.

Characteristics of the SJ (Ignatian) Temperament

The SJ persons have a deep sense of obligation and always want to feel useful. They want to be givers rather than receivers. Charity and service come easy to the SJ. They are deeply committed to caring for those in need and desire to contribute to the good of society. Very practical, they have a work ethic, with a strong sense of tradition and continuity with the past; and they like order and hierarchy in society. They want to belong to a group and like ceremonies and ritual. They have a strong sense of history and a great respect for elders and customs handed down from the past. They are the great conservators and stabilizers of society. Incapable of refusing responsibility they are often over-worked. "If I don't do it, who will?" Suspicious of change except when clearly necessary they usually opt for the status quo and are conservative in their tastes and choices. They are great law and order people; for them titles are important, and the law is important. They are careful, cautious, thorough, accurate, and industrious. They make good administrators and take deadlines seriously. They will do routine jobs without protest as long as these tasks have value and meaning. They show a common-sense, practical approach to everything and may be said to live by the Boy Scout motto: "Always be prepared". They are the most conscientious of all the temperaments. They represent all the positive qualities of the traditional phlegmatic temperament.

Many SJ persons lean toward pessimism, firmly believing in Murphy's law that if something can go wrong, it surely will. They have a tendency to look on the dark side of life and to be prophets of doom and gloom. Therefore, they need to work at developing hope and trust to enable them to look on the bright side and become more optimistic. Persons of the other temperaments, especially the NFs, can help the SJs develop and deepen their hope and trust.

St. James, the leader of the conservative element in the apostolic church, was a typical SJ. He insisted that Christianity should keep faithful to the ancient traditions of the Jews. St. Matthew's Gospel is a typical SJ document with its emphasis on law and order and its stress on Jesus as the new Moses, the law-giver of the New Covenant. Matthew is also the Evangelist who constantly quotes texts from the Old Testament to show how Jesus is a continuation of the traditions handed down from the past.

Among the four dimensions of the Eucharist: Commemoration, Celebration, Anticipation, and Contemplation — the first dimension, Commemoration, appeals most to the SJ person. The homilist at Sunday worship should include the dimension of tradition and the history of salvation in every homily since 50% of the congregation on an average Sunday will be SJs. It is also suggested that every Liturgy Committee be mindful of the liturgical year and celebrate and commemorate the past events of the history of salvation in a way to reach and touch the SJs.

Ignatian Spirituality

The spirituality of the SJ Ignatian temperament is a carefully-organized regimen of striving toward a relationship with God. In a sense Ignatian spirituality is the opposite of Franciscan spirituality which depends upon spontaneity and openness to the Spirit. SJ persons prefer an orderly, well-planned agenda to follow and become upset when too many changes are suddenly introduced. Characteristically, SJs are militant in their opposition to the possibility of heresy and are strong in their fidelity to tradition.

As the historical dimension of the Christian faith is especially important for the SJ persons, they need to see the continuity between what we believe and practice today with what has been believed and practiced during the past twenty centuries of Christianity. If they can see the journey of faith as a spiral which again and again comes back to the same spot but each time at a higher level, the spirituality of the SJ person will be much enriched. They need the experience of both continuity with the past and new growth toward a previously selected goal. Mere adherence to the past leads to a static status quo where there is no promise of healthy advancement of any kind. A vibrant Ignatian spirituality, with its tendency toward intellectualism, will find a way to keep a good balance between all the values of the past and the new insights and graces that God wishes to pour out upon us each new day.

The concept that life is a part of a long journey of faith which began with the coming of Jesus to earth and which will continue until his return at the end of time is very much appreciated by the SJ temperament. SJs experience the history of salvation in the present by using their sense perceptions and sensible imagination to provide them with passage into the mysteries of Christ's life through the reading of the Scriptures. The SJ person employs his senses to relive in imagination and by observation the Scripture stories and then with his own innate sense of duty follows the admonition of Ignatius "to draw some practical fruit" by his service to others.

Ignatian spirituality is probably best expresed in the celebration of the Liturgical Year. Through the annual celebration of the events of the life, death, and resurrection of Jesus during the Church year, Christians not only commemorate the past events of history but actually make them present and operative for us today. This practice of celebrating the marvelous deeds of salvation history is not something original with Christians. It goes back to the Israelites in the desert after their deliverance from the slavery of Egypt. Besides the annual Passover celebration, Jews at the time of Jesus remembered God's wonderful deeds in a "Berakah" meal. Their faith was that whenever they took time to remember God's marvelous works of the past, they made that same God present to work similar deeds for them. Thus they made the past become alive and real. In the doctrine of the real presence of the risen Lord Jesus in our Eucharistic Celebration, Christians have extended this practice of the Jewish Berakah into the Christian Liturgy. This practice is especially understood and appreciated by SJ persons. Gratitude for past benefits is very much a part of the SJ temperament, and liturgical piety is an appropriate example of Ignatian spirituality.

Ignatian Prayer

The purpose of Ignatian Prayer is to try to make the Gospels and the Scripture scenes become so alive and real to us that we can make a personal application of the teaching or message contained therein. Therefore, in addition to COMMEMORATION, the other key word for this type of prayer is PROJECTION. We attempt to project ourselves into the original events so that we become a part of them.

The sensible imagination is used more fully in Ignatian prayer than in any other type of prayer. Ignatius suggests that we try to use all five senses during our imaginary journey back to the events of salvation history and into the life of Jesus. We should try to imagine not only what we would see but also what each of the characters involved would say, what the wood of the cross would feel like, the smells, and even the tastes presented (for example, of the bitter gall and sour wine given to Jesus). The purpose behind the insistence of St. Ignatius on this vivid recall of past events is to try to make the event as real as possible. We project ourselves back into the event and become a part of it. This does not mean that we necessarily project ourselves into the original characters but simply imagine ourselves as we now are but a part of the original event. By participating as affectively as possible, we are to draw some practical fruit for application to our present day situation. For example, in the parable of the Good Samaritan (Luke 10:25-37), one might imagine oneself in place of the priest who passes by on the other side of the road lest he become involved; or we could make another meditation using the Ignatian method to think of ourselves as the man who fell among the robbers. Or, we can think of ourselves as the good Samaritan. We try to imagine what we might say to each of the characters in the Gospel story and what they might say to us.

Another way of using Ignatian Prayer is to put ourselves in the place of the different people who came to Jesus to be healed. Instead of thinking of physical ailments, we might think of ourselves as being spiritually blind, spiritually deaf, spiritually paralyzed, or covered with the leprosy of sin, etc. We can imagine ourselves coming to Jesus, or being brought to Jesus, and then having him reach out, touch us, and heal our spiritual malady. Our imagination can make this very vivid, and with sufficient faith on our part, we can indeed experience a true spiritual healing as a result of this prayer. The events in the life of Jesus can become so alive and real that we experience the presence of Jesus here and now in our midst. Such an encounter with God is the purpose of Ignatian prayer.

In addition to making ample use of the sensible imagination, Ignatian Prayer is very structured and orderly. Altogether ten distinct points are given by Ignatius for each of the meditations. They are:

(1) Choice of Topic
(2) Preparatory Prayer
(3) Composition of Place
(4) Petition for Special Grace Needed
(5) See and Reflect
(6) Listen and Reflect
(7) Consider and Reflect
(8) Draw Some Practical Fruit
(9) Colloquy With God the Father,
      Jesus Christ, and the Blessed Mother
(10) Closing with the "Our Father".

After the meditation, our feelings are aroused to make a proper response to the presence of Jesus. This corresponds to the **Oratio** part of *Lectio Divina*. Then, we take time just to be quiet and experience any new insights that our Intuitive Function might present to us. Thus all four steps of *Lectio Divina* are practiced during Ignatian Prayer; and all four functions utilized.

Problems in Using Ignatian Prayer

Unless they have been trained and experienced in this way of praying and thinking, many SJ persons, as well as others, find it difficult. In the past the SJ person was content to use vocal prayers and traditional forms of prayer. As they are the sensible, practical, "salt of the earth" type of persons, they all too often follow without question the leadership of religious or secular authority. Since the use of sensible imagination has not been popularly taught and practiced in our churches for the past several centuries, many people, even the SJs, often find Ignatian Prayer difficult to master. However, once one becomes familiar with the method and has sufficiently developed and exercised one's imagination, most SJs will come to depend upon this type of prayer as their regular, daily method of praying.

Since the SJ is inclined to be pessimistic, frequent meditation or reflection on the Resurrection of Jesus rather than constant recall of the Passion and Death is recommended to the SJ. In the *Spiritual Exercises of St. Ignatius* an attempt is made to strike a balance between the positive and the negative. Equal time, a whole week, is given to the Resurrection as to the Passion and Death. However, the characteristic note of gloom and doom is found in the emphasis by St. Ignatius on sin, judgment, and hell throughout the first week of the *Spiritual Exercises*.

Another major problem in using Ignatian Prayer is its tightly organized structure. Persons with a strong "P" temperament are apt to be driven mad with all this structure. Therefore if they use Ignatian Prayer, it is recomended they feel free to change the order or omit any of the parts that do not appeal to them. However, persons with a strong "J" temperament usually take to Ignatian Prayer like a duck to water.

The SP temperament especially finds this tightly organized structure impossible to follow. People who have not been able to put order into their daily lives will probably have a hard time remembering the different steps of Ignatian Prayer. It is like learning to drive a car with a stick shift. The first time is difficult; but after a period of learning, it becomes second nature. Furthermore, adequate time must be allocated to the prayer exercise. We must not try to hurry the process, otherwise nothing happens and no value is derived from this form of prayer. Help from a leader trained in conducting the Spiritual Exercises will be very beneficial in making these Gospel scenes come alive.

A GROUP OF IGNATIAN TYPE PRAYER SUGGESTIONS

The Ignatian Method is to place oneself in the Biblical scene and to become a part of it by way of imagination. Ignatius suggests that we try to imagine what we might see, what we might hear, and what the persons in the scene might be doing. Always, at each point of the contemplation, Ignatius says, we must "try to draw some practical fruit from the reflection for our own life today." In other words, what changes or challenges does our reflection on the event furnish us? In using the following prayer suggestions, it is suggested that one use either the four steps of *Lectio Divina* or the ten points recommended by St. Ignatius.

PRAYER SUGGESTION #1: (Luke 10:38-42) Imagine yourself a friend and fellow-villager of either Mary, or Martha, or Lazarus. You happen to meet one of them in the village and you are told that Jesus of Nazareth is coming to visit in Bethany. You express an interest in meeting him, and you are invited to come the next evening to have dinner with them and Jesus. Close your eyes and try to relive in your imagination, with as many vivid details as you can, what your meeting and the ensuing conversation with Jesus would be like. Draw some practical fruit from it.

PRAYER SUGGESTION #2: You, a devout Israelite from Ephesus, are a stranger in Jerusalem on your first trip for the Passover. It is Good Friday morning; you find yourself caught up in a noisy crowd leading a man away to be crucified. You have never seen a crucifixion, so out of curiosity you follow the crowd to Calvary and find the man's name is Jesus of Nazareth. You are fascinated by the proceedings and by the conduct of Jesus. You stay until he dies. Close your eyes and in your imagination relive the scene and try to capture the impressions and conclusions you may have experienced. Draw some spiritual fruit for your own spiritual growth. What change is this experience going to make in your life?

PRAYER SUGGESTION #3: (Luke 24:13-35) You are one

53

of the two disciples on the road to Emmaus on Easter Sunday afternoon. Close your eyes after reading the Scripture passage and try to relive the whole scene from beginning to end. Draw some spiritual fruit from the experience. For example, invite Jesus to stay with you: "The day is nearly over. The night is at hand. Stay with us."

PRAYER SUGGESTION #4:   (John 21:1-19) Imagine that you are Peter. Read the story very carefully so that you will remember all of the details. Then close your eyes and relive the scene in your imagination. Try to capture your feelings when Jesus asks you three times, "Do you love me?" Then answer the way you would want to answer rather than merely repeat what Peter said. When Jesus tells you: "Follow me," try to imagine what that might mean in the immediate future of your present life.

PRAYER SUGGESTION #5:   (Luke 10:25-37) Read the parable of the Good Samaritan and try to imagine yourself, first of all, as the priest who passes by on the other side of the road. What reasons could you give for refusing to get involved? Then try to imagine yourself as the person who fell among the robbers and who was left half-dead by the side of the road. What might you think as you see people pass you by and refuse your cries for help? Thirdly, imagine yourself as the Good Samaritan. Try to envision some situations today where you could act as a Good Samaritan to others in trouble.

PRAYER SUGGESTION #6:   (Mark 9:14-29) Read the story. Imagine yourself as the father of the possessed boy and apply the conversation between Jesus and the father to your own situation. Instead of an afflicted son, imagine the affliction is some fault of yours which has resisted cure. Bring this affliction to Jesus and ask him to cure it.

PRAYER SUGGESTION #7:   (Luke 7:36-50) Imagine yourself as the penitent woman who comes to Jesus in the house of Simon the Pharisee, washes his feet with her tears, and dries them with her hair. Try to imagine why you should be weeping and how you came to be convinced that Jesus would understand and show mercy. Imagine your reaction when you hear him saying to you, "Many sins are forgiven you because you have loved much."

PRAYER SUGGESTION #8: (Luke 4:1-13) Put yourself in the place of Jesus, imagine yourself being tempted in the same way as Jesus. How might you respond? The temptations of Jesus are suggestions that he misuse his newly-received powers to serve himself rather than use them for the benefit of others. He could change water into wine for the benefit of a newly-married couple, or multiply loaves and fishes to feed a hungry multitude in the wilderness, but he must not change stones into bread for his own use. Similarly, he could walk on water and calm the storms at sea for the benefit of others, but he must not cast himself down from the pinnacle of the temple to show off his power over nature. He could use his power over people to teach them about the Kingdom of God but never to make himself their king and ruler. We too have been given special powers. We must not use them for our benefit but always to help others. What can we do to make sure we follow Jesus' example when we are tempted to abuse the power God gives us?

PRAYER SUGGESTION #9: (Mark 8:27-38) Jesus' Galilean Crisis. Jesus is half-way through his public ministry. The people are beginning to abandon him (John 6:66). The Pharisees and religious authorities are plotting his death. Everything for which he has been working seems lost. Jesus leaves Galilee and goes into the pagan territory of Decapolis. He becomes aware that Isaiah 53 foretells his fate. He is seriously tempted to run away from his vocation. When he shares this with the apostles, Peter tries to dissuade Jesus: "God forbid that any such thing happens to you." Jesus turns on Peter in anger: "Get behind me, you adversary. You are trying to make me trip and fall. You are not judging by God's standards but by man's" (Matt 16:22-23). Put yourself in the place of Jesus or Peter. How would you react in a similar situation? What can you do to accept more willingly the crosses and disappointments in your present life?

PRAYER SUGGESTION #10: (Mark 14:32-42) Agony in the Garden. Jesus is still struggling with the destiny to which his Heavenly Father has called him. "O Abba, you have the power to do all things. Take away this cup of suffering from me." He looks for comfort and sympathy from Peter, James, and John but finds them asleep. Identify with Jesus in his agony. Recall some instances in your own life when you felt abandoned both by God and your friends. Through this identity with Jesus you will find the grace and strength to abandon yourself to God: "Not my will but thine be done."

PRAYER SUGGESTION #11: (Mark 10:46-52) Think of yourself as the blind Bartimaeus who hears that Jesus of Nazareth is passing. "Jesus, Son of David, have pity on me!" Jesus calls you over and asks: "What do you want me to do for you?" "Rabboni, I want to see." "Be on your way, your faith has healed you." We all are spiritually blind. We so often miss the obvious. We are blind to the needs of others. We are blind to our own faults and sins. Say to Jesus, "Rabboni, I want to see." Jesus lays his hands on you and you experience healing. Your eyes are opened, and you see that to which you had previously been blind.

PRAYER SUGGESTION #12: (Mark 10:17-31) Imagine yourself the rich young man who asks Jesus, "What more can I do?" Jesus hears your request and challenges you to go and dispose of everything you own, and give it to the poor, and then come and follow him. Would you have the courage to do this if you knew Jesus were asking this of you? Or would you turn away like the rich young man because you are still attached to the things of this world? It is hard to say whether we would act like the rich young man or like Peter who exclaims: "We have put aside everything to follow you!" But by using our imagination to project ourselves back into this Gospel scene, we should be able to discern where we now stand. Then, pray for the grace to follow Peter.

PRAYER SUGGESTION #13: (Luke 15:11-32) Read the story of the Prodigal Son; try to place yourself in turn as the younger son, as the elder brother, and then as the father. Try to think of times in your life when you have acted as each of the three characters. What opportunity might you have in your present life to follow the example of the father of the prodigal son?

PRAYER SUGGESTION #14: (Luke 16:19-31) Let us put ourselves in the place of the rich man in the story. Think of times when we have passed by the beggars who lay at our gate. Think of the times we have feasted sumptuously while half of the world's population starved. "Remember that you were well off in your lifetime, while Lazarus was in misery. Now he has found consolation here, but you have found torment." God forbid that we will ever have to hear these words from our Lord and Judge. What do we need to change to avoid hearing these words? To make this change of heart more real, try to relive as vividly as possible the Gospel parable to the very end, imagining that you are the rich man who has neglected Lazarus the beggar.

PRAYER SUGGESTION #15:   (Luke 18:9-14) Put yourself in turn in the places of the Pharisee and the Publican. Does your ordinary prayer resemble that of the Pharisee or of the Publican? What changes are needed to make your prayer more in accord with the teachings of Jesus and the example of the Publican? Imagine yourself as the Pharisee standing in the front of the church on a Sunday morning praising and thanking God that you are not like the rest of the people or like some poor wretches you know. Does this resemble any experiences in your own life? Does your prayer ever fall into the category of the prayer of the Pharisee? How can you become more like the Publican?

CHAPTER FIVE

AUGUSTINIAN PRAYER AND SPIRITUALITY
THE NF TEMPERAMENT

In this book we have given the name Augustinian to a very popular type of prayer which appeals especially to the NF temperament. St. Augustine, in whose honor it is named, was an NF (Intuitive-Feeler). One of the best known of the early Christian Fathers of the Church, he developed rules of spirituality for the monasteries of monks and convents of virgins in North Africa. These became models for the rules and constitutions of the majority of religious congregations of Western Christianity. The Augustinian method of prayer and spirituality was adopted and used by the Fathers of the Church and many other spiritual masters down through the centuries. The long history of usage and success of this type of prayer is probably due to the fact that the majority of the canonized saints seem to be of the NF temperament.

In Ignatian Prayer, where the key word is PROJECTION, one is projected back into the biblical scene by using the **sensible imagination** to become affectively a part of the original event and then to draw some practical fruit for our life today. The key word to describe Augustinian Prayer is TRANSPOSITION. In Augustinian Prayer, one uses **creative imagination** to transpose the words of Sacred Scripture to our situation today. One tries to imagine (intuit) what meaning the words of Scripture would have if Jesus Christ, or God the Father, or the Holy Spirit appeared and spoke them to us at this moment. In Augustinian Prayer we try to think of the words of the Bible as though they were a personal letter from God addressed to each one of us. Only secondarily are we concerned about the original, historical meaning of a text of Scripture; our primary concern during Augustinian Prayer is trying to discern what meaning these revealed words have for us today. Thus the Word of God becomes alive and applicable to our situation. For example, consider the words God addressed to the people of Israel in Isaiah 43 and imagine they are being spoken to you now: "Thus says the Lord Who created you and formed you: 'Fear not, for I have redeemed you; I have called you by name, you are mine . . . You are precious in my eyes and glorious, and I love you . . . fear not, for I am with you.' "

Transposing the ancient words of the Bible to the situation of the present is a practice that goes back to New Testament times. Jesus himself transposed the words of the Hebrew prophets to the situation of his own time. The Gospel narrators, St. Paul, and the other New Testament writers used transposition to apply the words of the Old Testament to the situations of the first century of the Christian Era. The Church Fathers of both the East and the West used this method of updating the Bible to find a way to relate its meaning to their time. Throughout the course of Christian history, saints, mystics, spiritual masters, spiritual writers, preachers, and just ordinary persons have used this method of transposition to discover the meaning of God's word and God's will for themselves.

All temperaments find Augustinian Prayer meaningful and helpful; but those of the NF temperament are usually the most adept in using it. The NF person has the most highly developed Intuition and Feeling, which are the two psychological functions most used in this type of prayer. Sensation and Thinking are also used; but to catch the new insights applicable to ourselves in the words of Scripture the intuitive powers are especially needed. To personalize the message the Feeling Function must be activated; otherwise the words remain abstract and impersonal and will have no lasting effect upon our lives. Since the Dominant and Auxiliary Functions of the NF person are Intuition and Feeling, they usually find the greatest joy and benefit from using Augustinian Prayer.

Characteristics of the NF (Augustinian) Temperament

NF persons are usually creative, optimistic, verbal, persuasive, outspoken, good at both writing and speaking. They have a great need for self-expression and communicate with others easily. NFs are good listeners, good at counselling, good in resolving conflicts and making peace. They hate conflict and are unable to operate at peak efficiency when the situation becomes tense and strained. They like to have face-to-face encounters and are able to read faces and catch non-verbal communications. NFs have deep feelings and are upset if treated impersonally. They find it difficult to handle negative criticism, and become discouraged when meeting a negative attitude in others, but blossom under affirmation. They freely give and need strokes and communicate their own enthusiasm to others. They need acceptance, support, and prefer cooperation rather than competition.

NFs are highly committed to helping others and usually relate well to those who befriend them. They are enthusiastic, insightful, full of empathy, understanding, and compassion. They see in others possibilities for good that other temperaments do not perceive. Being person-oriented they are apt to have favorites; but persons are always more important than things. Because Thinking and Sensing are their Inferior Functions, NFs must make a special effort to be logical and correct in their thinking and to be aware of details and routine.

NFs are always searching for meaning, authenticity, self-identity. They have a great urge for perfection and wholeness and are quite idealistic. They have a hunger for integrity and are willing to make great sacrifices to attain it. Personal growth and development are necessities for both themselves and anyone for whom they feel a responsibility. They are the natural rescuers of those in trouble, and this leads to the danger of becoming too involved in others' problems. Both the giving and receiving of spiritual direction are high in priority for them. Therefore, the NFs usually make good spiritual directors who help others grow in spirituality and wholeness.

Even though NFs are only about 12% of the total population, as much as half of the persons who make retreats, frequent Houses of Prayer, and write about prayer and spirituality will be of the NF temperament. Self-improvement, self-development, self-actualization are at the top of the list of their priorities. NFs have a tremendous hunger and thirst for growth in their inner life; and for those who believe in God, this can be satisfied only in prayer, spiritual reading, contemplation. They experience a great need for periods of quiet and silence in order to make contact with their inner selves. "How can I become the person that I am supposed to be?" "How can I become truly real, authentic, and true to my own unique self?", are questions uppermost in the mind of the NF. NFs are happy and content only when they are convinced that their outer life is in harmony with their inner self.

Contrasted with the SJs who are frequently pessimistic about themselves and others, NFs usually are optimistic and able to see good in everyone. Because of their optimism and hope, they will make personal sacrifices to help others grow and find their way in life. The NF, like the NT, has that sixth sense which we call

Intuition. This makes them capable of seeing possibilities and potentials to which the SJ and SP may be blind. Sometimes this is
expressed as a psychic ability or as Extra Sensory Perception (ESP).

NFs will enter into a life-long process of "becoming" yet may
never reach the ideal of "being". As intuitives, they are never
content with the present but always striving to fulfill the unlimited
potential for growth that God has implanted in every one of us. A
great urge for truth, beauty, purity, perfection, wholeness is theirs;
and they often set such high goals for themselves that they are unable
to attain them. Because the NF is future-oriented, while the majority
of people (the 80% who are either SJ or SP) are present-oriented,
other temperaments often have a hard time understanding the NF's
dissatisfaction with the present and their constant desire for change.

The Spirituality of the NF Temperament

The NF needs to find meaning in everything. The NF wants to
know that what one does makes a difference; that each person can
make a unique contribution; that he/she is important; that God loves
each one of us unconditionally, as we are now, sins and all. The NF
needs to be assured of this every day in order to keep growing into a
deeper and more intimate relationship with God. Experiencing a
personal relationship with God is the one essential element of any
authentic NF spirituality. Therefore, daily prayer and quiet are a
"must" for persons of this temperament.

The NF derives a heightened sense of meaning from every
event and relationship by constantly seeking the hidden meaning of
things. Through Intuition and creative imagination, the NF is able to
give new meaning to life's experiences, a meaning beyond the mere
external event of the here and now. Whatever is actually present is
never quite sufficient for the NF. Totally untenable for the NF is the
thought that the visible, external, here-and-now thing or event is all
there is. There always has to be something better on the horizon, or
around the corner, if only one will search for it. Invariably this
"better" thing will be something of the inner world of the spirit.
Hence, the hunger and thirst for God and prayer that most NFs
experience.

Just as the SJ (Ignatian) temperament has a profound interest
in the past, the NF temperament has a keen interest in future
possibilities. NFs are the visionaries of the world. Persons of the
NF temperament try to anticipate new directions into which destiny

and the will of God are leading them and the world. From this temperament usually come the prophets who seek to read the signs of the times. NFs are the eschatalogical Christians who are open to the gifts of the Holy Spirit; and the dimension of ANTICIPATION is the part of the liturgy which most appeals to them.

Because the NF is always reading between the lines in order to catch the inexpressible, the spiritual, the hidden meaning, this temperament best understands symbols and their use in prayer and liturgy. Carl G. Jung defined "symbol" as an attempt to express the inexpressible. Symbols are the way God speaks to us; and we, to God. Since the full meaning and experience of God are limited by external signs or words, symbols are the touchstones which we use to reach a greater understanding of these realities. The parables of Jesus in the Gospel describing God and the Kingdom of God are typical NF symbols which attempt to illuminate something that cannot be literally expressed in human words. The NF, and the NT, with their strong and creative Intuition, best understand symbols; while the SJ and the SP, because they always want to be literal and factual, even with God, frequently have a hard time with symbols. By catching and meditating on the symbols that appear in a prayer period, God and the things of the Spirit become more real and meaningful for the NF. New insights into the nature of God and the relationship between God and oneself are thus attained. The NF's faith committment is thereby enhanced and strengthened.

A great many of the books on prayer found on the market today are written by NF persons and addressed especially to the NF temperament. Therefore, of all the four basic temperaments, the NFs are usually the best cared for spiritually; but they also need this special care, since without spiritual growth and development they wither, fade, and die just like a plant that is not watered, nourished, and tended.

Augustinian (NF) Prayer

Of all the temperaments, the NF needs more time in prayer and quiet meditation than any of the others. For the NF such time is not a luxury but a necessity as far as personal development and relationship with God are concerned. In prayer the NF will use all four functions of Sensing, Intuition, Thinking, and Feeling; but their Intuition and Feeling are used most. Never content with the superficial, external meaning of a Scripture passage or other spiritual reading, they constantly search for the fuller, richer meaning. "What do these words of Scripture mean to me in my present situation?" "What message is the Lord trying to convey to me in these ancient words of the Bible?" By using their Intuition in this transposition, the NF makes the Bible relevant to current personal and community problems and needs. Then the Feeling Function, activated by the grace of the Holy Spirit, personalizes and ratifies this newly-discovered meaning for incorporation into one's life.

In order to practice the Prayer of TRANSPOSITION, which we call Augustinian Prayer, the NF needs to open him/herself to one's creative imagination. Believing as we do that the biblical writers were able to penetrate the wisdom of God and bring a portion of this eternal wisdom down to earth, our Intuitive Function and our creative imagination are used to discover how to apply this wisdom to our situation. Since the wisdom of God is eternal and applicable to all ages and all situations, the NF transposition of the message of the Bible to the needs of the present generation has been a way of praying down through the ages. Such openness to the Holy Spirit involves a certain amount of risk and experimentation which should always be subject to continued discernment. Therefore, a spiritual journal, where thoughts and inspirations are recorded, is a great help to the NF not only in making the transposition of meaning to today's situation but also for reviewing the progress and validity of one's insights or inspirations. Usually good with words, both in speaking and writing, the NFs find journal keeping not a chore but a joy. They use the journal to discover the deeper meanings of life and to experience new spiritual growth. NFs agree with Cardinal Newman, who once said that he could pray best at the point of a pen.

To be fully effective, Augustinian Prayer should consist of a dialogue between God and oneself. This can best be accomplished by using the four steps of *Lectio Divina*. First we listen attentively to what God is telling us in the words of Scripture by endeavoring to read between the lines to discern the deeper meaning contained therein. Then we reflect prayerfully upon their meaning and try to apply this eternal wisdom to our situation today. Next we respond to God's word by appropriate personal feelings and dialogue. Finally, we remain quiet and still in order to be open to any new insights that our Intuitive faculty brings forth. The NF person will probably spend the most time on the last two parts of the prayer, wherein their Dominant and Auxiliary Functions of Feeling and Intuition are activated. For the NF temperament this type of prayer comes very naturally and quite easily. However, other temperaments, when using Augustinian Prayer, may need to use more psychic energy to activate their Intuitive and Feeling Functions. Therefore we suggest that they should be well rested and allow ample time for this type of prayer.

Since the life of the NF revolves around personal relationships, this will also be true in the NF's prayer life. The NF should endeavor to create a good, loving relationship with each person of the Trinity: a parental relationship with the First Person; a brotherly, friendly relationship with Jesus; a spousal relationship of love with the Holy Spirit. Saints may also serve as models for the NF, and reading the lives of holy, mature, self-actualized persons who have had a good relationship with God will help to foster a growth of love for God in the NF. Ikons, statues, and other representations of art, which express beautifully and symbolically a good relationship with God will also help the NF in prayer.

A GROUP OF AUGUSTINIAN PRAYER SUGGESTIONS

PRAYER SUGGESTION #1: Read Isaiah 43:1-5. Change the words, "Jacob" and "Israel", to your own first name. Try to imagine the Lord speaking these words directly to you. What meaning would they have for you in your present situation? Try to transpose the message from God to yourself today. What is the Lord talking about when He tells you, "Fear not." What fears do you have? Water and fire were the two great dangers which aroused the fears of ancient people; what are the greatest dangers you face in your life? What is the Lord telling you to do in time of danger? Imagine Jesus saying to you now, "You are precious in my eyes, and I love you." "Fear not, I am with you." How do you see this to be true in your own situation today?

PRAYER SUGGESTION #2: Read Hosea 2:16-22. Imagine God or Jesus speaking these words to you. What meaning would you derive from them? Change the words, pronouns, names, so that they apply to your present situation; and write the passage on a piece of paper. Imagine going to the mail-box and receiving today a personal letter addressed to you containing these words. What meaning would they have?

PRAYER SUGGESTION #3: Read the 17th Chapter of St. John's Gospel. Rewrite it so that it could be a prayer that Jesus might be praying for you personally at this very moment in your life. Change or omit whatever words or verses that do not apply to you. If you have a tape recorder, read the new prayer into it. Then listen to it. Close your eyes and imagine Jesus praying thusly for you today. Or, you might simply read it slowly to yourself; and imagine Jesus praying or speaking these words to you.

PRAYER SUGGESTION #4: Take the prayer in Ephesians 3:14-21 and change the pronouns from the second person (you) to the first person (me). Write out the new prayer so that it is a prayer for yourself. Then read it aloud several times. Recite it slowly; put as much meaning into the words as you can. Try to savor every word and phrase. What changes in your present attitudes does this prayer suggest to you?

PRAYER SUGGESTION #5: (John 14:1-16) Close your eyes after reading this passage and try to imagine Jesus speaking these words to you. What would they mean to you? Repeat those words of Jesus that have special value for you; savor them lovingly, joyfully. Try writing them down in your journal in order to impress them more deeply on your mind and memory.

PRAYER SUGGESTION #6: (Matthew 5:38-48) Read the passage slowly several times. Try to discern what meaning the words might have if spoken by Jesus to you at this very moment. Whom do you need to forgive? How might Jesus be asking you today to turn the other cheek, to go the extra mile, to give away your shirt as well as your cloak? Feel free to apply these words of Jesus to some other area of life besides material possessions.

PRAYER SUGGESTION #7: (Isaiah 54:4-14) Read the passage slowly a few times. Try to imagine God the Father saying these words to you. What meaning might they have?

PRAYER SUGGESTION #8: (Philippians 3:7-16) Put yourself in the place of a person in Philippi who received this letter from Paul. He is writing with you specifically in mind. He knows your situation quite well. How do the words apply to you?

PRAYER SUGGESTION #9: (Isaiah 58:2-14) Justice and charity to the poor are the most authentic forms of fasting. How far can these words of God apply to your life? What more can you do to share your bread with the hungry, shelter the oppressed and the homeless, clothe the naked? Try to imagine God saying these words to you today. What is He asking of you at this time in your life?

PRAYER SUGGESTION #10: (Micah 6:8) "You have been told, O man, what is good and what the Lord requires of you: Do right, love goodness, and walk humbly with your God." Consider how these three requests sum up your relationship with God and your fellow human beings. Imagine God speaking these words to you. Close your eyes and repeat them slowly over and over again. Try to apply them to your own situation. What is God asking of you?

PRAYER SUGGESTION #11: (Matthew 7:1-5) Imagine Jesus speaking these words to you today. How far do they apply? What is he asking of you? What changes is he asking you to make in your life?

PRAYER SUGGESTION #12:   (Matthew 18:21-35) "My heavenly Father will treat you in exactly the same way unless each of you forgives his brother from his heart." Think of the persons in your life who have hurt you by what they said, or did, or failed to say and do. Taking them one by one, try to forgive each one in your heart and pray for them. Do this again and again even though you may have already done it in the past.

PRAYER SUGGESTION #13:   (John 8:1-11) "Has no one condemned you?" "No one, Lord." "Neither do I condemn you. Go now and sin no more." Think of the faults you still have, consider them one by one. Think of the things that others criticize and find fault with you. Imagine them bringing you to Jesus to have him condemn you. Instead he says to you: "Neither do I condemn you. Go, sin no more." How would this make you feel?

PRAYER SUGGESTION #14:   (Matthew 25:31-46) "What you do to the least of my brethren, you do unto me." Who are the "least breathren" in your life? Who are the people that you consider beneath you? Alcoholics, drug abusers, terrorists, Communists ????? Mother Teresa of Calcutta speaks of the presence of Jesus in the "distressing disguise of the poor". What should you do or say in regard to them if you see Christ in each one of them?

PRAYER SUGGESTION #15:   (I Corinthians 13:4-8) "Love is never rude or self-seeking. There is no limit to its forbearance, no limit to its trust, its hope, its endurance." This is an ideal for which we must continually strive. Talk to Jesus about your failures in charity and ask him what he wants you to do. Put your own name in the passage each time the word "love" or "charity" is used. How authentic would such words be in your regard? What do you need to change to make them authentic?

PRAYER SUGGESTION #16:   (Philippians 4:4-13) "Rejoice in the Lord always. Dismiss all anxiety from your minds." This is a difficult ideal to accomplish, yet a goal toward which we should constantly strive. Dialogue with Jesus about how you might come closer to this goal.

PRAYER SUGGESTION #17:   (Colossians 3:12-17) "Whatever you do, do it in the name of the Lord Jesus." Pick out one of the virtues suggested here, one you would like very much to attain. Talk to Jesus about what you might do to attain it.

PRAYER SUGGESTION #18:   (Hebrews 13:1-21) "Love your

fellow Christians always.'' Why should you show a special love to other members of your parish community? Who might you love more than you now do? For whom do you not care? How can you change?

PRAYER SUGGESTION #19:   (I Peter 3:8-13) ''Do not return evil for evil. Return a blessing instead.'' Think about the times when you have returned evil for evil and the times when you have indeed turned the other cheek and returned good for evil. Talk to our Lord about how you might carry out the recommendation of St. Peter.

PRAYER SUGGESTION #20:   (I John 4:7-21) ''If anyone says he loves God yet hates his brother, he is a liar.'' According to Jesus and Sacred Scripture, it is a contradiction to try to love God while refusing to love one of our fellow human beings. Read this passage several times, reflecting on each verse to see how it relates to your practice of love.

CHAPTER SIX

FRANCISCAN PRAYER AND SPIRITUALITY
THE SP TEMPERAMENT

In the thirteenth century St. Francis of Assisi introduced a type of spirituality which is ideal for the SP (Sensing-Perceiving) temperament. St. Francis, who was probably an ESFP, exhibited all the marks of the SP temperament, which is characterized by an attitude of openness and willingness to go in any direction that the Spirit calls.

Since we seem to be living in an age of the kind of individualism typical of the SP, it is not surprising that a large number of those taking part in the Prayer Project during 1982 chose Franciscan Prayer as their favorite way of prayer. This was despite the fact that less than ten percent of those participating in the Project were of the SP temperament. According to David Kiersey, about thirty-eight percent of the general population of this country belong to the SP temperament. Hence, understanding this type and learning how to use and utilize Franciscan Prayer will be beneficial to a large number of people.

Characteristics of the SP (Franciscan) Temperament

SPs must be free, unconfined, and able to do whatever their inner spirit moves them to do. Therefore, it is important that the SP be dedicated to God so that this inner spirit is the Holy Spirit and not a merely human spirit or an evil spirit. SPs are impulsive and dislike being tied down by rules. They want to follow whatever impulse strikes them. Again, it is important that they be committed to doing God's will; for otherwise their free spirit can lead them far astray.

SPs love action and become easily bored with the status quo. They are crisis-oriented, good at unsnarling messes, and able to get things moving. They make good trouble-shooters, negotiators, diplomats. They have unlimited energy as long as the crisis exists and work best and most efficiently when it is necessary to respond quickly and dramatically. They are flexible, easy to get along with, open-minded, adaptable, willing to change their position. They are good as conciliators since in their view almost everything is negotiable.

They live very much in the present without concern either for the past or future. Neither yesterday nor tomorrow exist for a thorough-going SP. They are always looking for something new, new places to go, new things to do. They dislike practice and want simply to perform and act. They thrive on excitement, adventure, risk, challenge. They hunger for activity and enjoyment. Optimistic, cheerful, light-hearted, witty, charming, they live life intensively and are capable of unrelenting vigor when challenged and excited.

The air takes on a glow when an SP enters the room. They bring with them a sense that something exciting is about to happen. They are good entertainers and are usually the life of a party with an array of stories. They live life extensively, are able to survive setbacks, are only temporarily defeated. A marvelous example of an SP in fiction is the character of Rhett Butler in *Gone With The Wind*. Other modern examples would include Elvis Presley, Joe Nameth, the unsinkable Molly Brown, Jennie Churchill, and Lillie Langtry.

Franciscan Spirituality

Franciscan spirituality is very popular among ordinary people, those men and women of action who want and need to do things for others. Acts of loving service can be a most effective form of prayer; yet so often we neglect to think of this showing of fraternal love as prayer. If an SP has made a commitment to centering his/her life in God and in the doing of God's will, all these acts will be accompanied by a free-flowing, spontaneous, informal praising, and loving dialogue with God. Franciscan spirituality is very optimistic and sees the beauty, goodness, and love of God everywhere.

The whole of God's creation is a Bible for the Franciscan temperament. God speaks to them through every sense impression: all that they see, or hear, or feel, or smell, or taste. Yet, the books of the Bible, especially the Gospel accounts of the life of Jesus will have a special appeal for the Sensing-Perceiving person. St. Francis of Assisi understood the true meaning of the Incarnation and the teachings and example of Jesus perhaps better than any other follower of Christ. When one considers that a Sensing-Perceiving person like St. Francis makes contact with God primarily through their sense impressions, it would follow that since the Incarnation is the visible, audible, tangible presence of God upon earth, the SP could relate quite well to Jesus' life and his teachings through the parables. Therefore, the Incarnation of God in the life of Jesus is the center around which Franciscan life and spirituality revolve and coalesce.

Because of their impetuosity and generosity, SPs are fond of the "grand gesture" whereby they dramatically express their commitment to God. A beautiful and humorous example of this is when Francis of Assisi stripped off his clothes in front of the bishop and handed them over to his father. There are numerous examples of these dramatic, impulsive actions in St. Francis' life and in the lives of other persons of the SP temperament.

Ordinarily, SPs are not excessively concerned about either the past or the future. They are usually merciful and forgiving toward the past and optimistic and hopeful about the future. Their motto is **carpe diem** (seize the day); but if they are centered in God, this will not be in the way of the Roman Epicureans but in following the teaching of Jesus: "Do not be concerned about tomorrow. It will have troubles enough of its own. Sufficient for the day is the trouble thereof" (Matt 6:34). Since very often they are attracted to following some hero or heroine, they should take as their model Jesus Christ or his Brother, St. Francis of Assisi.

The SP does not respond well to the symbolic but is primarily interested in the real and literal. However, they are capable of great and heroic sacrifices for a worthy cause. Therefore, their generosity may result in untold sacrifices which other temperaments would be unable to endure. Once convinced of the value of a goal, the pursuit of it becomes play and not work for the SP temperament. The SP is willing to give up all ties to the present and wander off after some faraway ideal. Some of the most heroic and greatest saints and many missionaries, including St. Peter the Apostle and St. Mark, show the characteristics of this temperament in their works and deeds.

The Prayer Life of the Franciscan (SP) Temperament

Franciscan Prayer makes full use of the five senses and will be flexible and free-flowing. It is what we call "spirit-filled prayer", totally open to the presence and voice of the Holy Spirit present in each one of us. Since SP persons can see God in the whole of creation, they are able to make a fruitful meditation on the beauty of a flower, a meadow, a lake, a waterfall, a mountain, the ocean, or any event of nature such as sunrises and sunsets, the changes of the seasons, Spring, Fall, a fresh snow in Winter. When considering the life of Jesus, SPs will be more concerned about events rather than teachings of Jesus. The events surrounding his birth, his hidden life, his baptism, his miracles (feeding the multitude, walking on the water, supervising the miraculous catch of fish), his passion, death, and resurrection will hold special interest for the SP. The parables Jesus used are also apt to have a great appeal to the SP person.

If there is any temperament that can honestly claim that their work is their prayer, this would be the SP. Much of their prayer is what is called virtual prayer or the prayer of good works. Of all the temperaments they have the least need for long periods of formal prayer. While other temperaments may need as much as a whole hour of prayer time each day, the SP person functions well with 20 to 30 minutes of formal prayer in the ordinary working day. Nevertheless, they should try to give at least the minimum of time aforementioned to formal prayer daily while endeavoring in their own fashion to live in the presence of God, and thus be united with Him, throughout the day.

A prayerful SP will find that the thought of God predominates every waking moment. The famous Jesus Prayer: "Lord Jesus Christ, have mercy on me, a sinner," and other ejaculatory prayers are readily used by the SPs and enable them to live constantly in the presence of God and to see His hand in everything: in nature, in the events of divine providence, in other people, and in themselves. The Psalms, along with the Gospels, are usually the favorite Bible books of the SP. However, because of their enthusiastic nature which is so often filled with joy, praise, peace, and love, SPs should be encouraged to experiment with new forms and ways of praying which are not confined to the formal and traditional.

Since they usually have a great facility for spontaneous prayer, they may belong to a charismatic prayer group; but as the Spirit moves them, this membership may be on-again-off-again. In addition to praise, the aspect of the sacred liturgy which appeals most to the SP is CELEBRATION. They love to celebrate the goodness, greatness, love, and power of God. Once again, we go back to the possibility that this is a Franciscan Age since we see our present liturgies called Celebrations rather than the Sacrifice of the Mass they were called in previous times.

The Sensing-Perceiving person dislikes formal prayer and prefers a free-flowing, informal communing with God. When an SP makes a directed or long retreat, the retreat director should give persons of this temperament the freedom to do whatever strikes them, indicating however that they should share with the director all that occurs between them and God in the course of the day. If forced to follow a strict routine, such as the *Spiritual Exercises* of the Ignatian Retreat, SPs are apt to find it stifling. In fact, the routine will become simply maddening to them; so that they will either quit and go home or feel miserable for the duration of the retreat. To force this temperament into a strict schedule or rigid routine of prayer is a waste of time and totally unproductive of spiritual fruit. The more freedom in their prayer time, the more fruitful it is apt to be. Once SPs have made a decision to give themselves totally to God, there is simply no sacrifice that they will refuse to make; but it has to be in accord with the SP temperament and not according to the SJ, NT, or NF way of praying and living. A spiritual director or retreat master who fails to understand this and tries to force the SP into the same mold that other temperaments follow will accomplish little or no good at all and probably do some harm. The SP may give up the pursuit of holiness or give up the guidance of a director who fails to make proper allowance for the peculiarities of the SP temperament.

The SPs are best at short-range projects. They need to see quick or instant results. Therefore, any spiritual exercise which will show some worthwhile fruit in a short time should be chosen for them and by them. For example, they might be given acts of charity and ministry to others on a short term basis. Since they thrive on the visible, audible, and tangible, they love to work with their hands and with tools. During a retreat they may be given something which they can do with their hands: molding clay; painting a mandala; crocheting or knitting a banner, stole; or executing some other work of art. By way of relaxation during a retreat, an SP might assist around the grounds by doing some gardening or other physical activity. This answers their need for action and good works.

The SP loves to give and receive gifts and to see the reaction of pleasure and surprise in the receiver. They might be encouraged to use the arts and crafts to make things which can be given as gifts to others. At prayer, the SP will often show forth love for God by using a musical instrument, a paint brush, or anything that involves movement, action, and the senses. SPs have a strong appreciation of beauty and feel a need to produce beauty by their own efforts. St. Francis expressed this in the creation of the Christmas creche. Paper and pencil work is apt to be deadly and counter-productive for the SP, so a spiritual journal is not to be recommended. To relax the SP needs some less demanding activity like walking in the woods and taking time to observe and reflect upon the sights and sounds of nature.

Since the SP cannot tolerate long periods of silence, strict adherence to the *Thirty Day Ignatian Spiritual Exercises* is not recommended for this temperament. In consideration of their special needs, the rules for such a retreat need to be bent. If more than one SP is attending the retreat, they should be permitted to have periods of conversation together but not with the other retreatants. If they opt to follow the silence of the retreat, some challenge should be given them: a difficult goal which will be productive of short term, noticeable results. If it is challenging enough, the SP will spend untold hours of continuous perseverance on it.

A goal that might be suggested to the SP during a retreat or in spiritual direction would be that they strive to have the thought and will of God predominate every waking moment of the day so that they can see the hand of God in everything that happens. Once convinced of the value of such a goal, the SP will give him/herself no rest until it is attained.

A GROUP OF FRANCISCAN TYPE PRAYER SUGGESTIONS

The SP person may or may not find it useful to follow the four steps of *Lectio Divina*. However, when other temperaments use these SP prayer suggestions, it is recommended that the four steps of *Lectio Divina* be used.

PRAYER SUGGESTION #1: Take your crucifix, look intently at it, feel it, kiss it. In your imagination go back to the first Good Friday. Try to put yourself in the place of Jesus being nailed to the cross. This is what St. Francis did in the cave at Alverno near the end of his life. As a result he experienced the Stigmata, the actual wounds of Jesus, in his hands and feet. Try to imagine having the nails driven through your wrists and feet; try to feel the kind of stabbing pain Jesus must have felt. Try to identify with Jesus in his passion and crucifixion. Imagine yourself hanging suspended on the cross for three long hours, stripped of your clothing, naked before the jeering mob of people, wearing the crown of thorns, suffering in every pore of your body, suspended between heaven and earth.

Why this terrible pain and agony? Why this waste of human life? Jesus offered himself as a victim of love, offered himself to the forces of evil which were threatening to engulf the world at the time. Imagine these immense forces of evil as a giant river in flood stage sweeping across the face of the earth and destroying everything in its path. Jesus offered his fragile body to this immense power of evil and allowed its full force to be absorbed into his body. Returning good for evil, he absorbed the impact of these evil powers and thus neutralized their brunt and broke the back of evil in the world. (Read I Cor. 1:23-25; Gal 6:14; Phil 2:5-8; Isaiah 52:12 to 53:13.)

Today the floodgates of evil are again threatening to engulf and destroy the human race. A nuclear war could wipe away both the present generation and all future generations. God is looking for victims of love who will offer themselves as a sacrifice to these forces of evil in the same way that Jesus did. We need souls who are willing to make a commitment of love and sacrifice to God for the salvation of our brethren (cf. Isaiah 53). In this very serious period of history all of us need to take on something of the boldness of the SP. If we follow the example of Jesus, and our Brother St. Francis, we can hope to experience ultimately resurrection and perfect joy.

PRAYER SUGGESTION #2: Take a walk through the woods or fields or along the road and look for signs of God's love, beauty, power, wisdom, goodness, balance. Praise and thank God for revealing himself in all the events of history: in one's personal history, in the history of the world, and in the history of salvation. Think of some of the mysteries in God's creation which we cannot understand or explain — for example, the problem of sin and evil in the world. Try to make an act of blind faith and trust in God's wisdom, power, and love even when we cannot see clear manifestations of his wisdom, power, and love. Read Psalm 8.

PRAYER SUGGESTION #3: Read Daniel 3:26-90. Spend the remainder of the half hour composing your own canticle of praise of God for all the beauties of His creation. Include the beauties of the inner world of the Spirit, of one's own nature, of friends, as well as of the physical world.

PRAYER SUGGESTION #4: Think of the person in the world that you love the most. Ask yourself the following question: How can I see the presence of God in that person? Spend some time praising and thanking God for giving so much goodness, beauty, grace, etc. to that person. Spend some time thanking God for the gift of love whereby you are able to love that person and that person is able to love you.

PRAYER SUGGESTION #5: Think of the person that you least like of all your acquaintances. Try to see something of God's goodness, love, life, truth, beauty in that person. What might you do to foster and increase the presence of God in that person? Prayer is always a way to help another.

PRAYER SUGGESTION #6: Plan some sort of celebration of gratitude for God's gifts to some particular person or persons you know. It may be a birthday party for a member of your family. It can be something very simple — for example, invite someone for ice cream and cake some afternoon or evening. Make sure that the celebration is centered around praise and gratitude to God for His blessings, His goodness, His love. (Planning and executing this would be a typical Franciscan Prayer in action.)

PRAYER SUGGESTION #7: Go outside; look for two trees: one which resembles the kind of person you would like to be or your goal in life, another which expresses in some way the kind of person you see yourself to be now. Decide what you need to do in order to change from the way you now are to the way you would like to be or the way God would like you to be.

PRAYER SUGGESTION #8: Praise and thank God for all the good qualities that you find in yourself. How can you more fully develop these good qualities?

PRAYER SUGGESTION #9: Watch a beautiful sunset or sunrise. Contemplate the waves of the ocean, a mountain lake, a waterfall, a tree, a leaf, a bee, a beetle, an animal. If you have a telescope, look at one of the planets, especially Saturn or Jupiter. If you have a microscope, study a leaf or a crystal of some sort. As you contemplate God's creation, try to come to a better appreciation of God's beauty, power, goodness, love, wisdom.

PRAYER SUGGESTION #10: Plan an act of charity for someone in need; then endeavor to carry it out, either alone or with the help of others.

PRAYER SUGGESTION #11: Visit someone sick or old in a nursing home and talk to him/her about God. Before you leave, pray with this person and ask God to bless and help him/her. If you do not know anyone ill or aged who lives nearby, simply go unannounced to some nursing home and ask permission to visit some patient who seldom has visitors.

PRAYER SUGGESTION #12: Write a letter of consolation or condolence to someone who has lost a dear friend in death or who is presently suffering some tragedy in his/her life. Be sure to talk about God in the letter and close with a prayer, perhaps Ephesians 3:14-21.

PRAYER SUGGESTION #13: If you have available Beethoven's "Ninth Symphony", listen to the Third Movement. (This was the dying request of Pope Pius XII after he had received the last rites of the Church. He wanted to die listening to this very beautiful and peaceful piece of music.) Listen to any other piece of classical, non-vocal music that you find uplifting and spiritual. Other suggestions: Fourth Movement of Beethoven's "Fifth Symphony", "Third Piano Concerto" of Beethoven, "Love Death of Tristan and Isolde" by Wagner.

PRAYER SUGGESTION #14:   Read slowly Cardinal Newman's poem, "Lead Kindly Light", reflecting upon the meaning of each of its phrases. Try to discover a way of applying the words to your own life. (Cardinal Newman wrote these words on the boat coming back from Rome when he was earnestly striving to discover the direction God's light was leading him.) Sing the song several times, and then throughout the rest of the day hum its tune as you go about your duties. Sing it again before retiring.

PRAYER SUGGESTION #15:   Read aloud Francis Thompson's poem, "The Hound of Heaven", or have someone read it aloud to you while you listen. Try to identify with as much of it as you can. How has God pursued your soul like a hound that never gives up? How have you tried to shake off his pursuit of you? What do you need to do now to surrender yourself completely to Him and His will? Read once again the pertinent stanzas of the poem.

CHAPTER SEVEN

THOMISTIC PRAYER AND SPIRITUALITY
THE NT TEMPERAMENT

We have given the name Thomistic to the NT type of prayer, not because it was the only method of prayer recommended by St. Thomas Aquinas, but because it uses the syllogistic method of thinking known as the Scholastic Method which was popularized by Aquinas and his followers. The main emphasis in this type of prayer and spirituality is on the orderly progression of thought from cause to effect. Close attention to the process of rational thinking is required in order to arrive at an appropriate conclusion. Therefore, those persons who have not developed the discipline of logical thinking will usually find this type of prayer very unprayerlike. They will see it more as study and reflection rather than real prayer. However, if the total method of this prayer, as we suggest it, is used; and the four steps of *Lectio Divina* (**Lectio, Meditatio, Oratio, Contemplatio**) are followed, all four psychological functions will become involved. Thus it will be real prayer and not an exclusively intellectual exercise.

Since the time of Descartes the predominant philosophy of the Western World has been rationalism. These past four centuries have been a field day for the highly intellectual, speculative, rational persons of the NT temperament. Since persons of this temperament, by their very nature, are frequently in positions of leadership in the community, it is easy to understand how this form of prayer came to be recommended above all others in the post-Tridentine period of Church history. Even most of the Jesuit masters of spirituality adapted the *Spiritual Exercises* to the rationalism of the age. This form of prayer and spirituality was propounded by most Catholic writers from the seventeenth century to the middle of the twentieth century. Most books of meditation written during this period followed the rationalistic approach to prayer.

Indeed there is a place for this type of prayer, not only for the 12% of the population who are of the NT temperament, but also to some extent for all of us. We need a certain amount of exposure to this discursive, reasoning form of prayer. It is highly recommended for use when reflecting upon a virtue or fault and when trying to discover how best to practice the virtue or overcome the fault. It is especially recommended to be used as a method of prayer in preparation for the Sacrament of Penance and Reconciliation.

Characteristics of the NT (Thomistic) Temperament

Persons of the NT temperament possess a very logical mind which approaches a problem with an orderly movement of thought from cause to effect or from effect back to its cause. They gravitate to anything complicated, exacting, or challenging to the mind. NTs have a great thirst for truth and for the freedom that flows from a knowledge of the truth. They have a tremendous desire to understand, comprehend, explain, predict, and thereby control the realities with which they live. The NT wants to master and excel in whatever he/she attempts, be it sanctity, business, church administration, etc. They feel compelled to rearrange the environment and are usually leaders in whatever occupation they choose for themselves. The NT has a tendency to be a perfectionist and is alert to his/her own failures as well as to the shortcomings of others. In the mind of an NT the worst faults are stupidity and incompetence. The NTs hate to repeat an error. They are even impatient with the initial error; to repeat it becomes anathema. They ruthlessly criticize themselves and others who do not live up to the high standards they have set. Because the NT often has a sense of inadequacy coupled with a great fear of failure, he/she often is subject to self-doubt and is unduly demanding of him/herself. NTs tend to be workaholics, scheduling even their play time as they do their work, demanding that they should "have a good time". They must excel even in the games they play and are apt to be poor losers. Very competitive they try to avoid all mistakes.

Because Feeling is usually the Inferior Function of the NT, this temperament has a tendency to be impersonal when in relationship with others. Communication with others tends to be terse, precise, logical, with a reluctance to state the obvious. However, they are usually quite straightforward so that one always knows where one stands with them. They are often oblivious to others' emotional responses, insensitive in inter-personal relations, and tend to be unaware of how much their cold impersonal way of acting affects and hurts others. In the presence of a strong NT, others may feel that they do not count. To develop Feeling which is their Inferior

Function, membership and participation in a larger group will help NTs experience the emotional level of the community and by its contagion develop and express their own feelings and emotions. Hence, the great need of NTs for good liturgical celebrations.

Because of their native intelligence and well-developed intuitive abilities, NTs are frequently in positions of leadership. Therefore their influence on the community is considerably greater than one would assume from the fact that this group is only 12% of the general population. Many lawyers, architects, planners, general consultants are of the NT temperament. NTs delight in planning not only their own life but also the lives of others. Very future-oriented, regarding the past as dead and gone, for the NT what matters most is what might be.

The NT is fascinated by power, not only power over people but power over nature, over ideas, over the future. They have a burning desire to be able to understand, predict, explain, and control every reality. This desire for power is the secret motive behind their intense need for competency and behind the life and actions of many NTs.

The desire for competency gives the NT a compulsion to improve and become better than they now are. David Kiersey states: "The NT badgers himself about his errors, taxes himself with the resolve to improve and ruthlessly monitors his own progress. He continually checks the pulse of his skills and takes his conceptual temperature every hour on the hour. He must master understanding of all objects and events, whether human or extra-human, physical or metaphysical, in whatever domain he stakes out as his area of competency" (*Please Understand Me*, p.49.). Because the NT is so serious about learning new knowledge, skills, and competencies, he frequently gains outstanding proficiency in his field of endeavor. What the NT sets out to do, he/she usually does quite well.

Thomistic (NT) Spirituality

The Thomistic approach to spirituality is similar to the approach which the modern physicist or scientist uses in solving a scientific mystery. For example, the NT recognizes it takes much time and effort to investigate the causes behind one's lack of self discipline and to take the necessary steps to attain the sought virtue. Therefore, an NT will set goals for him/herself and will systematically proceed with them. Every fiber of the mind will be challenged to attain the self-discipline to conquer laziness, pride, and selfishness and to center one's life in God and in loving service to others. A logical, step-by-step approach will be the preferred instrument in the NT's total arsenal of spiritual weapons to conquer self-will and submit one's life to the will of God.

The NT prefers neat, orderly forms of the spiritual life as contrasted with the free-spirit, impulsive attitude of the SP. This attitude of the NT is not sufficiently appreciated in today's permissive society. Yet, one's spiritual growth must be a balance of both; for one needs both the seriousness of purpose of the NT and the outpourings of emotion which are characteristic of the SP.

The spirituality of the NT temperament will be centered in an earnest pursuit of all the transcendental values: truth, goodness, beauty, unity, love, life, spirit. With their tremendous hunger for perfection, once they have made a choice of God and holiness as their ultimate goal, NTs are willing to exert superhuman effort and energy to attain this goal. An excellent example is St. Teresa of Avila who, from what we can deduce from her life and works, seems to have been an NT. Once she had chosen sanctity, nothing could stop her pursuit of it.

In accord with the NT's desire for competency, the NT temperament seems to have an especial attraction for the higher mansions of spirituality. St. John's NT Gospel has always been the favorite Gospel for mystics and contemplatives. NTs are aware that contemplation is a grace and gift from God but leave no stone unturned in their cooperation with the graces of God that are offered to them. Because of their disdain for second-best, they seek total truth and authenticity in their own life and work hard to reach the whole truth about themselves, about God, about sanctity. This intense search or pursuit of the truth colors their whole spiritual life.

Thomistic (NT) Prayer

The type of prayer most suitable to this temperament is the logical, rational, discursive meditation whereby the intellect leads one from one proposition to another until a logical conclusion is drawn in the form of some resolution or ethical demand. All four steps of *Lectio Divina* should be used in Thomistic Prayer; but the main emphasis will be on the orderly progression of thought from cause to effect during the **Meditatio** portion of the prayer. The **Lectio** portion may or may not involve a direct reading of the Bible but may simply begin with some point of revealed teaching of the Bible further developed by theological reflection. Thus the subject for Thomistic

Prayer may be some virtue recommended or some fault condemned by divine revelation. However, Thomistic Prayer is not complete when it is confined solely to the rational consideration of a virtue, fault, or religious practice. One needs to respond with feeling and personal involvement to the intellectual consideration and thus involve the heart as well as the head. Also one must pause and remain still mentally to allow one's Intuitive Function to contribute new insights or inspirations. Thus, all four functions of Sensing, Thinking, Feeling, and Intuition will be activated during Thomistic Prayer. But always the major thrust will be on the role of Thinking and Intuition, since these are the Dominant and Auxiliary Functions of the NT.

In accord with the NT's search for truth, the Thomistic prayer method earnestly seeks to attain the whole truth about the subject chosen for consideration. One looks for new insights from God concerning the virtue to be practiced, the fault to be overcome, the religious practice to be perfected. In books on prayer, the Thomistic method of prayer is frequently called "discursive meditation". Emphasizing and exercising the mind, will, and intuition, it uses Feeling and Sensing somewhat secondarily. Sensing must be used to collect the needed data upon which one will meditate; while the Feeling Function is used to personalize and intensify the resolutions resulting from the reflection upon the selected topic. Feeling is also needed to avoid any Pelagian attitude of imagining that sanctity can be attained simply by grasping the truth and willing oneself to follow it.

In this type of prayer, one takes a virtue or fault or theological truth and "walks around it", studying it from every possible angle. To enable one to get a full grasp on the topic chosen for Thomistic Prayer, it is recommended that one *uses* the seven auxiliary questions: WHAT, WHY, HOW, WHO, WHERE, WHEN, WITH WHAT HELPS and applies each of them to the topic selected. For example, one might take the virtue of faith as the subject for one's meditation. One would then ask the following questions: What do we mean by faith? What is entailed in the practice of faith? What are the reasons to justify the pursuit of faith? Why should I have faith? What is the value of it? How might I practice faith? When and where should it be practiced? Who are some of the people in the Bible and in history who are examples of the practice of faith? Finally, what aids can I use to help me practice faith? The whole exercise would conclude with suitable resolutions of how one is going to practice the virtue of faith. Traditionally, the proponents of this type of prayer recommend that we take some short scriptural phrase or some other appropriate saying as a "spiritual bouquet", which is repeated through the day as a centering or ejaculatory prayer. The purpose of this "spiritual nosegay", as it is sometimes called, is to continue throughout the day the prayerful reflections begun during the early morning meditation.

Unless our discursive reflections during the prayer period result in a change of behavior, they would not be considered authentic Thomistic prayer. "Metanoia" or conversion is an essential element of Thomistic Prayer. A logical step from the new insights into truth received during the meditation is to make the necessary changes in one's life. This would be the practical fruit expected from each exercise of Thomistic Prayer and expressed through one or more resolutions adopted at the conclusion of the discursive meditation.

The Place of Thomistic Prayer in Today's World

Thomistic Prayer and discursive meditation have fallen on hard times in the post-Vatican II church. Part of this is a normal reaction against its over-emphasis during the long post-Tridentine period of history and the Age of Rationalism. When we emphasize one side of a truth too much, the pendulum usually swings to the opposite side of a wholesale rejection of this exaggerated truth. However, we should be very careful lest we lose an important part of our heritage. There is indeed a place for this type of prayer and spirituality, not only for the 12% who are of the NT temperament, but also for all of us. We all need a certain amount of exposure to this discursive form of prayer. The proper balance will be attained if we use the four steps of *Lectio Divina*. In this way all four functions, Sensing, Thinking, Feeling, and Intuition, will be exercised; and all the temperaments will be able to find some value in it.

One of the main reasons for the present bias against Thomistic Prayer, especially on the part of older priests and nuns, is the fact that formerly in seminaries, convents, and novitiates, this was often the only form of prayer recommended and taught. Because very few of the seminarians or novices belonged to the NT temperament, most of these young people were unable to endure a steady diet of this type of prayer. Many of them came to the conclusion that, because of their inability to use Thomistic Prayer fruitfully, they were not among the chosen ones called to sanctity or to the higher mansions of prayer and spirituality. This was indeed unfortunate. Instead of the guilt engendered because of the many distractions and dryness during the practice of this type of prayer, this should have been seen as the authentic rebellion of one's inner being against the imposition of a wrong form of prayer and spirituality. The mistake was trying to place all beginners in this very structured, NT method of prayer. As one progresses in bringing all the functions into conscious, balanced use, the Thinking Function will grasp and utilize this way of praying. Many of the respondents in the Prayer Project who were clerics, nuns, or religious indicated they were at first quite adverse to this style of prayer; but once into it they were pleasantly surprised by the benefits reaped.

There is always the danger that this method of prayer becomes an impersonal and objective research or study project and that, although clear thinking is used the emotions and feelings are neglected. NTs, and all of us, need to be reminded that, in addition to intellectual conviction, our keen desires must be motivated by love of God. Unless we feel attracted to a teaching because of our love for God and His Will, we will never be motivated to put it into practice. One needs to enter into a prayerful, personal dialogue with God in order to obtain the needed grace and love to carry out our resolutions. Hence, the need of using **Oratio** and the Feeling Function in Thomistic Prayer.

In response to the questionnaires during the Prayer Project in 1982, a great number of the respondents, both lay and religious, expressed a definite bias against Thomistic Prayer. This is somewhat understandable in view of the fact that only 8% of the participants were of the NT temperament. For most of them, Thomistic Prayer did truly require extra psychic energy to activate their lesser used functions. Therefore, we suggested that it should not be used every day but reserved for those times when one is well rested and has plenty of energy to give to it. Then, it will be found a most rewarding type of prayer which will make a substantial contribution to one's spiritual growth.

A GROUP OF THOMISTIC PRAYER SUGGESTIONS

Thomistic Prayer is not meant to be exclusively an intellectual exercise, "a head trip". Besides using our intellect and common sense (practical judgment) to discern exactly what is Christian teaching, we should also use our heart to get in touch with our feelings and emotions. Unless we are attracted to a teaching in the Bible, we will not be motivated to put it into practice. Intellectual conviction indicates the direction our life should take to become Christ-like; but two other elements — God's grace and our love and desire — are essential to pursuing it. To obtain God's grace, a prayerful dialogue with God the Father or Jesus or the Holy Spirit should be a part of every Thomistic Prayer. Then we must find some way of arousing our feelings of love and desire so that we are willing to put forth the needed psychic energy to carry out our resolutions. In each suggestion of Thomistic Prayer, apply the auxiliary words: what, why, how, when, where, who, with what helps.

PRAYER SUGGESTION #1: (Luke 1:26-38) Consider and contemplate the faith of Mary, who is a great saint primarily because of her faith. Faith means the total commitment and blind trust of our lives into the hands of God. We can understand the meaning of faith by seeing it exemplified in the life of another person. Write down the qualities of Mary's faith as you see them exemplified in the Annunciation. What changes do you need to make in your life in order to bring your faith more into conformity with Mary's faith?

PRAYER SUGGESTION #2: (Luke 1:39-46) Consider the ministry of Mary toward her cousin Elizabeth. Without any thought of herself, Mary unselfishly hurried to the aid of an old woman having her first baby and remained there until after the birth of John. Mary may be seen as the first "Eucharistic Minister" bringing the flesh and blood of Jesus to the home of Elizabeth and Zachary. What might we do to minister better to the needs of others?

PRAYER SUGGESTION #3: (Mark 9:33-37) Spiritual Childhood: virtues of simplicity, trust, charity, purity of intention. What does

Jesus mean when he says that we must become as little children if we wish to enter the Kingdom of Heaven? What are the qualities of a small child that are especially needed in our relationship with God? Which of these qualities do you need to intensify and develop at the present time in your life? If possible, read the chapter on "Spiritual Childhood" in *The Autobiography of St. Therese, The Little Flower.*

PRAYER SUGGESTION #4: (Mark 8:34-38) Doctrine of the Cross. What does Jesus mean when he insists that in order to be his disciple we must take up our cross and follow him? What are the crosses in your present life? Are you carrying them in the same way that Jesus carried his cross to Calvary? What do you need to change in your present attitude toward your crosses?

PRAYER SUGGESTION #5: (Matthew 10:39) "He who seeks only himself brings himself to ruin; whereas he who brings himself to nought for my sake discovers who he really is." What does Jesus mean by the words "bring oneself to nought for my sake"? What do you need to do in your life to put Jesus' concerns ahead of your own? How does self-discipline enable us to "discover who we really are"? Just who are we really? What is our primary purpose on earth? Is it to satisfy ourselves or to fulfill some God-given destiny? What is the ministry God is asking of us?

PRAYER SUGGESTION #6: (Matthew 5:20-26 and John 2:13-17) What is the difference between the anger of Jesus and the anger which Jesus condemns in this passage from Matthew? Why is anger so wrong that Jesus equates it with the command against killing? St. Thomas defines anger as the desire to attack violently anyone who poses a threat to something we consider valuable. What about self-defense of our country, our family, ourselves? How far are we justified to go to defend ourselves? Is the anger you sometimes feel a justifiable anger, similar to that of Jesus, or the kind of anger Jesus condemns in the Sermon on the Mount? What does one do about one's anger?

PRAYER SUGGESTION #7: (Matthew 6:26-34) Study carefully each verse of Jesus' teaching about Divine Providence. With what of it do you agree? What do you consider not applicable to your present way of life? What justification can you make for the verses you are unwilling to accept literally? What changes do you need to make in your life in order to follow Christ's teachings here?

PRAYER SUGGESTION #8: (Matthew 6:19-25) How does this

teaching of Jesus differ from the generally accepted practice and teaching of today's world? How far are you willing to go to follow Jesus in his teaching about true riches? In what ways are you trying to serve two masters? In your life who are the different masters determining what you do; how you act; where you spend your time, money, energy? What practical changes do you need to make in your present life in order to bring it more into accord with the teaching of Jesus?

PRAYER SUGGESTION #9: (Matthew 5:23-24) "If you bring your gift to the altar and there recall that your brother has anything against you, leave your gift at the altar, and go first to be reconciled with your brother, then come and offer your gift." Are you willing to take this command of Jesus literally? Do you believe that it is more important to be reconciled with your brothers and sisters than it is to go to Mass on Sunday? At present is there anyone in your life who is not reconciled with you? Have you tried to become reconciled with him/her? Have you tried as much as you should? As much as God would want you to do? Do you really love that person who is not reconciled to you? What more can you do to become reconciled with those who have something against you? Even if the "thing against you" is not real (i.e. imaginary), is there anything you should do to bring about an understanding between the two of you?

PRAYER SUGGESTION #10: (Matthew 13:44-46) "The Kingdom of God is like a treasure hidden in a field, which a man finds and rejoicing goes and sells all he has in order to buy the field." Where have you discovered the hidden treasure of the Kingdom of God? Are you willing to sell everything in order to possess it? Have you disposed of everything else in order to obtain it? Do you sufficiently appreciate the hidden treasure of God's Kingdom? What do you need to do to appreciate better this "hidden treasure", "this pearl of great price"?

PRAYER SUGGESTION #11: (Mark 10:35-45) Read the passage carefully. Notice that Jesus in no way condemns ambition but simply teaches the disciples that their desire to be first should be in the area of humble service to others. "Whoever wants to rank first among you must serve the needs of all." Do you have this kind of ambition? What do you need to change in your present way of life in order to do a better job of serving others? How might you, like Jesus, give your life in ransom for others?

PRAYER SUGGESTION #12: (Matthew 11:29; Luke 14:7-11; I Corinthians 4:7) Take the virtue of humility. Reflect upon it. What does it mean? What is the connection between humility and authenticity? What does Jesus mean when he says, "Learn of me because I am meek and humble of heart." If you have some good spiritual book, you might read what it says about the virtue of humility. Think of some examples of persons in the Bible who were humble (Moses, Mary, Joseph). Where have you been humble in the past? What are some examples of your failure to be humble? What changes do you need to make in your life in order to be more humble? What do you need to do in order to grow in humility? What might you do this day to practice humility? End the period of prayer with petitions to God, Jesus, Mary, and the saints to help you to be more humble.

PRAYER SUGGESTION #13: (Mark 15:10; Acts 13:48) Consider the fault of envy. Reflect upon its meaning. St. Thomas defines envy as the evil sadness one feels at the success of a rival or peer. Have you ever felt envy? When? Why? What did you do about it? Have you ever suffered as a result of the envy of someone else? What did you do about it? How was envy the cause of the death of Jesus? Why do people experience envy? Why are envious people often unaware of their envy? How might you discover whether you still harbor secret envy toward others? What might you do to avoid being envious of others? How is love the opposite of envy? End the period of prayer with fervent petitions to God asking Him to help you discover your secret envy and to help you overcome it.

PRAYER SUGGESTION #14: (Philippians 2:4-8) "Your attitude must be that of Christ." What does St. Paul say is the attitude of Christ? (We must empty ourselves.) What is there within me that needs to be emptied? St. Paul says that we must take the form of a servant or slave. What exactly does this entail in my attitude toward those with whom I live, work, associate? What changes do I need to make in my life in order to bring it more into conformity with that of Jesus? What steps do I need to take to bring about a more Christ-like attitude toward myself, toward others, toward God? End the period of prayer with fervent petitions to God for the grace to carry out whatever resolutions your conscience has revealed during the reflections upon this text of Philippians.

PRAYER SUGGESTION #15: (James 2:14-26) Virtue of Charity. What efforts am I making to serve the poor, the suffering, the needy people of my community? What am I doing for the poor and needy and suffering people of the world? Do I really believe that they are my brothers and sisters? What in the area of charity can I do to fulfill Christ's command to love others as He has loved us? "Faith without works is as dead as a body without breath."

ONE MAY TAKE ANY VIRTUE OR FAULT AND USE THE THOMISTIC METHOD TO REFLECT AND PRAY OVER IT FOLLOWING THE MODEL SUGGESTED ABOVE IN PRAYER SUGGESTIONS #12 AND #13.

CHAPTER EIGHT

USING OUR SHADOW AND INFERIOR FUNCTION IN PRAYER

One of the many marvels of creation is that, in endowing human nature with the four psychological functions of Sensation, Intuition, Thinking, and Feeling, God created humans in such a way that they are capable of perceiving and operating at the level of physical reality as well as at the numinous level of the spirit. Each of the four functions is like a swinging door which can swing out to relate to the external world of physical reality and inward to relate to the inner world of the spirit. However, the four functions operate differently when relating to the transcendental level of reality than when relating to the obvious physical world. In fact, they perceive and operate in an opposite fashion. The function which is Dominant when coping with the external, conscious world will be the Inferior Function when dealing with the inner, transcendental world; and vice-versa, the function which is Inferior in external world usage will be the Dominant Function when concerned with the inner world of the spirit. The Myers-Briggs Type Indicator measures our relationship with the outer world and our actions and reactions as we respond to it. Therefore, following the laws of complementarity, the opposite of our MBTI score should give us our hidden inner temperament, which is called the shadow.

The MBTI scores have been so arranged that the four preferences on the left side (Extraversion, Sensing, Thinking, Judging) deal primarily with the external, physical world while the four preferences on the right side (Introversion, Intuition, Feeling, Perceiving) deal primarily with the inner world of the spirit and only secondarily with the outer, physical world. This would be in accord with the recent discoveries concerning the left side and right side of the brain. Actually, all eight preferences deal with both worlds but it is a matter of primary and secondary choices. In each instance the secondary choices will require from us somewhat more psychic energy in order to activate them. They, in turn, become our Inferior and Tertiary Functions or Attitudes. Also, these secondary choices become a part of our shadow and are the function and attitude which the unconscious half of our nature most often uses in its operations.

An understanding of the above paragraph will explain why Introverts, Intuitives, Feelers, and Perceiving persons usually have an easier time at prayer than do Extraverts, Sensers, Thinkers, and Judging persons. Prayer is when we make contact with the inner world of the spirit where God dwells. However, we must not forget that our unconscious self, our shadow, is the opposite of our conscious self. Therefore, if Extraverts, Sensers, Thinkers, and Judging persons take the time and extra energy to activate and develop their shadow and their inferior functions and inferior attitudes, they can have as great, or even greater, experiences of God and the inner world of the spirit, which includes such transcendental values as truth, goodness, beauty, justice, love, life, freedom, unity, psychic energy. The inner world of the spirit may become so familiar to Introverts, Intuitives, Feelers, and Perceivers that sometimes they overlook and miss the obvious. Ultimately no one temperament or personality type has a corner on the prayer market or the inner spirit world. For all temperaments and types the secret to a successful prayer life and healthy relationship with God is to make the effort to attain and maintain a good balance in the use of all four functions and all four attitudes. This will be accomplished by discovering and working with our shadow and by activating the transcendent dimension of each of the four functions, especially the Inferior and Tertiary Functions.

When most people think of their shadow, they consider it something negative and evil, something to be avoided and hidden rather than brought to the light of prayer. According to Carl G. Jung, who first coined the term "shadow", 80% of the shadow is gold ore waiting to be dug out of the depths of our unconscious and put to work in our conscious life. In his later writings Jung identified the shadow as the unconscious half of our human nature. This unconscious side of the human psyche, which is the source of all that is best as well as all that is worst in an individual or society, contains both primitive, undeveloped, inferior qualities and an unlimited, unrealized potential for good. The shadow is psychic energy within our soul waiting to be brought into consciousness and put to good use in the service of God, our fellow human beings, and ourselves.

During the first 25 to 30 years of life, one should concentrate upon training and developing one's Dominant and Auxiliary Functions. After the age of 30, one should begin to develop more fully one's Inferior and Tertiary Functions. This is when one begins to deal seriously with one's shadow. A good way to begin the process of using one's shadow in prayer is to read the portrait of the temperament and type that is directly opposite to one's MBTI score. For example, if one's type is INFP, then one's shadow will be similar to the ESTJ portrait as it is described in the Kiersey-Bates book, *Please Understand Me* and by Myers-Briggs in *Introduction to Type* and *Gifts Differing*. One can presume that the things decribed in this opposite temperament and type are part of the qualities of one's positive shadow which have remained somewhat undeveloped and unconscious.

In adulthood one should attempt to activate these qualities of the shadow and bring them into some sort of balance with the qualities of one's conscious life which were developed earlier. The shadow becomes negative and evil only when that part of it which Divine Providence wills to become conscious is repressed and denied conscious expression. God gives us sufficient psychic energy each day to handle that part of the shadow which is ready to be gathered into consciousness and put to good use. The daily, formal period of prayer and meditation is a perfect time to make contact with that part of the shadow which is ripe for harvesting. By activating the transcendent dimension of each of our four functions, especially our Inferior and Tertiary Functions, we become capable of handling the fresh, psychic energy which is released each time we uncover a portion of our shadow. In Appendix II of this book, we offer some suggestions for recognizing and discovering each type's shadow and some ideas on how to use one's shadow in prayer. (For a further discussion of Shadow, see Chapter Eleven, "Our Shadow Always Follows Us", in *Arise: A Christian Psychology of Love*, by Michael and Norrisey.)

The Transcendent Dimension of the Inferior Function

In his writings Carl G. Jung frequently talks about the "transcendent function" of the human psyche. By this he meant the tendency of the four psychological functions to be both conscious and unconscious thus unifying physical realities with inner, spiritual realities. In this book we prefer to limit the use of the term "function" to the four functions of the MBTI. Instead we prefer to speak of the **"transcendent dimension"** of each of the four functions. By this we mean that ability of Sensation, Intuition, Thinking, and

Feeling to make contact with the metaphysical, spiritual levels of reality such as God, the soul, truth, goodness, beauty, unity, freedom, love, etc. and shed illumination on them through a unifying symbol so that they are incorporated into our consciousness. During prayer we seek to activate the transcendent dimension of each of the four functions since there is much grace and unconscious psychic energy at each of these four doorways to the inner world of the spirit. Special attention, however, should be given to the activation of the transcendent dimension of the Inferior and Tertiary Functions (the functions with which we have the least proficiency) since, according to Jung, most of the undifferentiated psychic energy lies concealed behind these two doorways in the unconscious spiritual areas of life. It is here we will find our shadow.

In *Jung's Typology* Marie Louise von Franz states: "The inferior function holds the secret key to the unconscious totality of the person." Therefore, if we wish to attain wholeness, maturity, sanctity, we need to work especially with our Inferior and Tertiary Functions. Because they are hidden in the deeper realms of the shadow, we frequently neglect to develop them. We reach wholeness only when we are willing to engage in the effort and discipline necessary to bring about a working relationship between the Ego (the focal point of our **conscious** life), the shadow (the **unconscious** depths of our inner self), and God. Only when a good partnership between these three is established will we reach the destiny for which we were created. The purpose of daily prayer and meditation is to attain this working relationship.

The Inferior Function always has a mysterious quality because of its unconscious contents. While being the weakest spot in the armor of our conscious life, it is nevertheless the depository of great unconscious potential; but until this potential is brought to the surface of consciousness, it remains undifferentiated: i.e., able to go either in the direction of good or in the direction of evil. When the Inferior Function is denied or rejected, we get along tolerably well until some unexpected eruption of the shadow overtakes us. Then we can expect trouble because, when neglected, the Inferior Function tends to become negative and teams up with the evil elements of the shadow.

By becoming consciously aware of our Inferior Function, we can undertake its transformation and reduce its compulsive eruption and awkwardness. During the second half of life, after we have somewhat mastered the use of our Dominant and Auxiliary Functions, we can expect frequent manifestations of the emerging Inferior

Function. If we develop its potential, we will create a whole new world of possibilities and a whole new outlook on life for ourselves. When the Inferior Function is allowed to operate without our conscious control, it is like opening a Pandora's box. The contents of the unconscious spill out helter skelter. On the other hand, if we repress or deny the Inferior Function, we keep the door closed to the riches lying buried in the unconscious. By acknowledging our inferior qualities, we open ourselves to pain, suffering, struggle, and conflict; but the incorporation of our Inferior Function into consciousness will lead to the wholeness and balance which is the mark of a mature person.

Generally we are very touchy and easily hurt when the deficiencies of our Inferior Function are pointed out to us. In this area, whether it is Sensing, Intuition, Thinking, or Feeling, we are the most uncertain of ourselves. We have no tight rein of conscious control over the Inferior Function as we do over our Dominant and Auxiliary Functions, and so the Inferior Function will often express itself in highly emotional, erratic, or infantile behavior. It comes and goes as it likes and marches to an unconsious drummer. When used, the Inferior Function is generally slow, cumbersome, unadapted and requires a great outlay of psychic energy which quickly exhausts us. Frequently we find ourselves crucified between the Inferior Function and the Dominant Function, which often tries to thwart and by-pass our weaker functions by playing to our egocentricity. The Inferior Function is our greatest problem and our greatest challenge.

Everything in the unconscious earnestly seeks and desires to become conscious. However, in the plan of God there is a proper order and time for each element of the unconscious to become conscious. If we would open at once all four doorways of Sensing, Intuition, Thinking and Feeling to the unconscious, our conscious life would soon be flooded out or overwhelmed. This condition is called a psychosis. These doors must be opened gradually, one by one, and entered. The hour set aside for prayer or meditation is the ideal time to make contact with the inner, spiritual, unconscious areas of life. Prayer, then, can be called the active use of our conscious faculties to foster the proper and easy entrance of the psychic energies from the unconscious shadow into our ordinary life and activities. A more traditional way of saying the same thing would be to say that prayer is the exercise which puts us in contact with the Spirit of God dwelling within our inner being.

Even those in the higher mansions of contemplative prayer must use their conscious faculties during prayer to make contact with the Holy Spirit. Non-believers in God, even though they may call it meditation or some other such word, must also rely upon what we call prayer to make contact with their inner psyche. The activation of the transcendent dimension of all four functions will enable us to make contact with the psychic powers and energies of God and spirit. Using the Inferior and Tertiary Functions during the time we set aside for prayer and meditation will give us some of our most valuable faith experiences because a new dimension of practice will allow us to see God and inner realities in a different way. To a similar but somewhat lesser extent, everything we have said about the Inferior Function can also be said about the Tertiary Function.

How do we discern which of the four functions is our Inferior and which is our Tertiary? In Appendix II we make it easy for you by giving the different functions in ascendancy for all sixteen types of human personality. In *Gifts Differing* Isabel Briggs Myers explains the process for discerning these different functions from your MBTI score. Also, there are several questions one can ask oneself to help determine one's Inferior Function. Which function most exhausts me when used extensively? When do I require absolute peace and quiet in order to operate well? When am I most easily disturbed by distractions? Which is the most difficult to use when tired? When am I most often negative, and where do I make the most mistakes? Where am I the least confident? In scanning the qualities of each of the functions as they are given in Appendix I, which one lists my shortcomings? Whichever function occurs most often as your response to the above questions will probably indicate your Inferior Function. The second most frequent response will be your Tertiary Function.

Activating the Transcendent Dimension of the Sensing Function

The transcendent dimension of the Sensation Function is activated by one's sensible imagination; and, if properly used, both Franciscan and Ignatian Prayer methods will accomplish this. By using active imagination we open the doorway to our shadow and allow some reconciling symbol to appear. In a flash, this symbol may reveal a new dimension of God or a new insight into one of the facets of our faith or of our relationship with God. Through sensible images, comparisons, analogies, and parables we are led to a better understanding of the mysteries of God.

For example, contemplation of the beauties and powers of nature may open the doorway to some symbol or insight that will help us understand a mystery of God. A memorable experience of this can be had on a visit to the Niagara Falls. Standing at the bottom of the Falls, close to the powerful waves of water sweeping over and down, one appreciates more fully the infinite power of God. The thought comes: "All of this mighty power I am seeing and hearing here is only a drop in the ocean compared to the power of God." The time at the bottom of the Falls becomes a beautiful and powerful experience of faith-filled awe and prayer that stays with one for many days thereafter.

Something similar can happen when one watches a sunset or sunrise. A sunrise is a daily symbol of birth and new life, while each sunset can be a symbol of death. If one is attuned to the grace of God while observing these phenomena of nature, one understands a little better one's relationship to life and death and the promise of resurrection. The amazing thing is that one can watch a thousand sunrises and sunsets and each time the symbolism of life and death becomes more alive and meaningful.

A new understanding of God and the transcendentals also occurs when one listens to a beautiful piece of music, or watches the ocean waves, or contemplates a snow-covered mountain. Modern photography, especially slow motion, easily activates the transcendent dimension of Sensing. With some effort, we can activate the transcendent dimension of all five of our senses: seeing, hearing, touching, tasting, smelling; and thus the Sensing Function becomes the doorway through which a spiritual insight into the inner world becomes consciously present.

Interestingly enough, people whose Tertiary or Inferior Function is Sensing usually have an easier time activating the transcendent dimension of this function. When Sensing is the Dominant or Auxiliary Function, one tends to get lost in the welter of sensible details and sense impressions that bombard one. Whereas, when Sensing is the Inferior or Tertiary Function, the tendency is to cut through and ignore extraneous details, and go to the very heart of the reality. Instead of being distracted by too many details, one quickly and easily sees the inner beauty, power, order, harmony, wholeness of God shining through His creation. Whether contemplating the macrocosm of the physical universe or the microcosm of a single cell this will be true. With some special effort, however, those whose Dominant or Auxiliary Function is Sensing can learn to activate its transcendent dimension and use it well during prayer. A Sensing person, who will do a rote action, for example, saying a rosary, listening to a waterfall, dabbing paint on a canvas or other object, will find that this continuous, almost rhythmic, sense-overload will often trigger one's active imagination into a contemplation of the mysteries of God or one of the transcendental values.

Activating the Transcendent Dimension of the Intuitive Function

Of the four functions, the transcendent dimension of Intuition is probably the easiest to activate in order to get in touch with the inner world and the transcendent realities of God and spirit. Since the basic purpose of Intuition is to catch the symbols that rise from the unconscious, to use it during prayer may be comparatively easy; but if this is the Dominant or Auxiliary Function, one must develop the ability to cut through the many extraneous symbols and recognize the really important ones.

Intuition apprehends those symbols or images which tie together opposite poles of truth. Intuition discovers the synthesis that maintains the balance between thesis and antithesis. This in turn is productive of new energy and grace. By using one's creative imagination, a balance is established between the conscious and unconscious, between the physical and spiritual, between God and creation, between nature and grace.

The transcendent dimension of Intuition opens the veil hiding the future from us, enabling us to read the signs of the time and discern the future directions and the future possibilities of our life. Time, leisure, and patient waiting will allow the creative imagination to produce the inspiration that gives new insights into God and our relationship to God. Intuition enables us to discern God's will for ourselves and others for both the immediate and distant future, to see God's providence and loving care, and to experience the untapped potential for good that has not yet been actualized in ourselves and in the community.

Because of the modern prejudice in favor of the physical and rational and against the spiritual and metaphysical, those who have Intuition as a Tertiary or Inferior Function may be wary and afraid of it and thus find it difficult to activate its transcendent dimension. The important thing is to give due consideration to any sudden insights that seek one's attention. If they are neglected and not taken seriously, they become lost in the welter of sensible images which fill our daily life. These inspirations need to be caught on the fly since they quickly come and go. If we fail to take hold of them when they are fleetingly presented, they pass by and are lost. To retain them it is advisable to write them down as soon as they appear.

One of the best ways to begin to use or develop the transcendent dimension of Intuition is to pay attention to one's dreams. Dreams are the voice of the unconscious which reveals itself to us every night. Dream language is always the language of symbols, and we need our Intuitive Function to discern their meaning. Dreams should be regularly and conscientiously jotted down in a notebook which is kept ready at the side of one's bed. They should then be taken to prayer and reflected upon to discover any insight which will enable us to understand better one or the other of the transcendental values and thus deepen our relationship with God and our inner self.

Those who do not remember their dreams can use other methods to activate the creative imagination during waking hours. Simply to spend a day in devotional fantasy with the Holy Family or with Jesus in his public ministry is a way to activate one's creative imagination. Another method is using guided imagery with or without music. In Initiated Symbol Projection (ISP), which usually requires the help of a guide or friend, a common universal symbol of the Collective Unconscious is projected into an imaginary activity of the participant. Developed by psychologists in Europe at the end of World War II, ISP does not require highly trained professionals and can be undertaken with the aid of anyone who has a well-developed Intuition. This person should also be trustworthy and sincerely concerned for the welfare of the other. This person, however, should be familiar with the process so that one can be lead through the different symbol projections. (See Roberto Assagioli, M.D., *Psychosynthesis*, Viking Press, 1971, pp. 287-303.)

The Augustinian method of prayer is the best type of prayer to activate the transcendent dimension of Intuition. The emphasis here is on discovery of some symbol or insight that makes a spiritual truth more real in our life. We may come to understand how to reconcile two opposite truths or values — for example, justice and mercy, truth and compassion for the sinner, gentleness and severity, confrontation and non-violence, etc. We should also reflect upon the symbols used in our Christian religious practices, especially in the liturgy, e. g., the Incarnation which unites God and human nature or the Paschal Mystery which ties together death and resurrection. Through the use of the transcendent dimension of Intuition we will find new meaning in these expressions of our faith.

Activating the Transcendent Dimension of the Thinking Function

Through the transcendent dimension of the Thinking Function

we come to a deeper understanding of God's truth and justice in relationship to us and in our relationship to God. When Thinking is operating at a transcendent level, it grasps the unifying symbol which ties together apparently contradictory and opposing truths. One is enabled to simplify complex issues and make them undertandable to others in simple terms. Thinking works both at the conscious level and the unconscious level, but it cannot work simultaneously at full force at both levels. We must slow down the conscious level of thinking and give the mind the needed leisure to allow the unconscious, transcendent dimension of Thinking to operate. Once this happens, we will be surprised at the sudden creative insights that allow us to see a common denominator which brings together a whole series of disparate facts or truths.

When Thinking is the Inferior Function, it can have a powerful influence during prayer when its transcendent dimension is activated. Rather than becoming lost in a labyrinth of individual truths, a unifying symbol or truth brings many truths together. In other words, we are able to simplify a complex issue containing diverse truths and perceive something that unites them and bridges the differences between them. In turn, this unifying symbol becomes a new experience of truth which brings delight to the one receiving it and clarification and enlightenment to others. A synthesis of the total is obtained without all the extraneous facts and details. A person with a Dominant Thinking Function may denigrate this but will have to admit that, simplistic as it may seem, a plausible but logical conclusion has been reached nevertheless.

The Thomistic type of prayer can be used to activate the transcendent dimension of the Thinking Function. The purpose of Thomistic Prayer is to delve deeply into revealed truths and allow recognition of the reconciling or unifying symbol that will bring together the apparently opposite poles of truth. Reading and studying Scripture themes, reflecting on doctrine or ethics, considering one's attitude in an examination of conscience are ways of activating the transcendent dimension of the Thinking Function. For example, one might consider the problem of how and why an all-powerful, all-loving, all-good, all-wise God allows so much evil in the world and our own part in it. If we succeed in activating the transcendent dimension of Thinking, we may receive an insight into these apparently contradictory realities. This sudden enlightenment into the truth brings joy, freedom, and peace. "You shall know the truth and the truth shall make you free" (John 8:32). Because Thomistic Prayer makes use of both Thinking and Intuition, it is a most valuable source of new insights into the truths of God, the world, and our religion.

Activating the Transcendent Dimension of the Feeling Function

The transcendent dimension of the Feeling Function helps one to experience the transcendental values of goodness, love, and mercy in a personal way and not as a mere impersonal tenet of belief. The Feeling Function penetrates external appearances and acknowledges the value and worth of the inner person, be it God, Jesus, or another human being. Rationalists, tyrants, and oppressors, who treat others as chattel or objects to be bought, sold, and used as one would an animal or inanimate object, ignore this dimension of personhood. But, once we have grasped this personal dimension of another, we will respect the other's freedom, dignity, and independence.

Through the transcendent dimension of Feeling we make God, Jesus, and the Holy Spirit living persons, who are just as real as the human beings with whom we associate. This in turn enables us to experience the giving and receiving of love between God and ourselves. When Feeling is the Dominant Function, the problem with its use in prayer is that one is overwhelmed with a host of different feelings. Whereas, when the Feeling Function is the Inferior or Tertiary Function, it is often easier to filter out what is really important and apply it to one's relationship with God without being drowned in a sea of confusing emotions. When we activate the transcendent dimension of the Feeling Function, we know instinctively the direction into which God's will is calling us and respond accordingly either by gentleness or severity, tolerance or confrontation, justice or mercy.

At the conscious level Feeling operates through love, joy, peace, patience, gentleness, generosity. At the unconscious level the Feeling Function picks up the mood and feelings of an individual or group and the vibrations of the unconscious, spiritual powers, including God. Therefore, those who have repressed or neglected to use their Feeling Function will be helped in the activation of their feelings at a transcendental level by participating in large or small assemblies such as prayer or faith sharing groups. For example, a good experience of communal liturgy will enable them to release their Feeling Function.

Four methods of prayer — Augustinian, Franciscan, Ignatian and Benedictine — can activate the transcendent dimension of the Feeling Function. Thomistic Prayer also may be used if care is taken to add the recommended **Oratio** and **Contemplatio**, the colloquies and aspirations. One might say that activating the transcendent dimension of the Feeling Function is the basic goal of all prayer, since the purpose of prayer is to establish a personal relationship with God, Jesus, and the Holy Spirit. This is what religion and prayer are all about — to bring us to an experience of a union of love with the person of God. If we open ourselves to the graces of the Spirit of the Lord, realizing and working with the four psychological functions and attitudes will bring forth a whole new dimension of relationship, knowledge, and understanding not only of ourselves and others but also of the transcendental values and God.

CHAPTER NINE

TEMPERAMENT AND LITURGICAL PRAYER

When considering God and the things of God, we are dealing with inexpressible, numinous realities that are transcendental to the physical world in which we live. We have no literal way of describing these spiritual realities and so we are forced to rely on metaphor, comparison, analogy, or images which we call symbols. Therefore, any relationship with God on earth will necessarily involve the use of symbols, which are the sensible means by which the transcendentals express themselves in our conscious life. Jesus constantly used symbolic language in his attempts to tell us about God and our relationship with God. Some examples of the symbols used by Jesus in his teaching would be calling God "Abba" or "Daddy" or using metaphors like "kingdom of God", "heavenly banquet", "sower and seed", "mustard seed", "treasure hidden in a field". The parables of Jesus are extended symbols of God and our relationship with God. Symbols can be audible (the words of Sacred Scripture), visible (the community of believers at a Eucharistic celebration), tangible (the crucifix), tasteful (the bread and wine of the Eucharist), or olfactory (the smell of burning incense).

In addition to individual symbols we also use a series of symbolic events to express the process of our becoming united with the life of God and to explain the practice of our religious beliefs. We call this a myth. Unfortunately, many people think a myth is a mere legend, existing only in the imagination and without objective reality. According to Webster's Dictionary this is a secondary meaning for myth and is not the meaning we are using here. Through ritual or liturgy, a myth is told again and again in order to bring the life of the community into harmony with the life of God. The best known Christian myth is the Paschal Mystery which relives the whole process of life, death, and resurrection. The Eucharist is the ritual which we use to relive and make real this Paschal Mystery. By repeating the story of the Paschal Mystery again and again, the

103

community of believers becomes a part of the process of death to the old and resurrecion to a new and more transcendental level of life.

A myth becomes alive, active, effective, and productive of new grace and new psychic energy through the collective, living symbols which are activated in the minds and hearts of those listening to or participating in it. The main purpose of public liturgical services is to make these collective symbols come alive. When a congregation comes together to relive the myths of their religious history, the symbols and rituals used in the liturgy must be effective and real so that the present members can become a part of the history of salvation and thus make the myth a part of their lives.

Authentic religious symbols can be either dead or alive, depending upon whether or not the symbol is able to move minds, wills, feelings, and lives. For a great many Christians today the symbols used in the liturgy are no longer living symbols and therefore no longer affect or change their lives. There is a big difference between a dogma of faith in which we believe and a living symbol of the faith which we experience. Dogma is a rational attempt to describe the object of our faith, while a living symbol gives us an experience of God. Symbols put life into the dogmas of faith so that they become real and meaningful. Because different human temperaments apprehend symbols in a different way, depending upon which function is Dominant and Inferior, a knowledge of temperaments will greatly aid in the task of restoring life to our religious symbols and our liturgies.

The Symbols of the Eucharist

The Holy Eucharist was instituted by Jesus Christ to give Christians the opportunity to be united with God on earth just as Jesus was united with his Heavenly Father during his life on earth. For Christians the Eucharist is the principal way to establish and maintain this contact with Jesus and, through Christ, with God during the in-between times marking the interval between the first coming of Jesus to earth and his final coming. This Eucharistic union with the Risen Lord is accomplished by means of four living symbols: COMMUNITY, WORD, CROSS, MEAL. These four symbols respond to the four psychological functions of Feeling (Community), Thinking (Word), Sensing (Cross), and Intuition (Meal). To experience the presence of the risen Lord through these four symbols, the transcendent dimension of each of the functions must be activated. Otherwise, the particular symbol that corresponds to that function will remain lifeless and useless to the participants in the liturgy.

The four symbols also respond somewhat to the spiritual needs of the four basic human temperaments. The experience of community appeals especially to the SP (Franciscan) temperament. The Word of God excites the interest of the NT (Thomistic) temperament with its search for truth. The vivid reliving of the Cross fascinates the historically-conscious SJ (Ignatian) temperament. The eschatological dimensions of the ritual meal challenge the future-oriented NF (Augustinian) temperament. A well-conducted Eucharistic liturgy thus presents four different ways for the congregation to experience the presence of the Risen Jesus. (1) We *celebrate* the real presence of Jesus through the coming together of the *community* of believers. "Where there are two or three gathered together in my name, there I am in the midst of them" (Matt 18:20). (2) We *contemplate* the *Word* of God from the Sacred Scriptures. St. Augustine says that when we proclaim the Word of God in the Eucharist we are just as much in the presence of the Holy Spirit as we are in union with Christ when we partake of the Eucharistic bread. (3) We *commemorate* the Pachal Mystery of the *Cross*. "Every time you eat this bread and drink this cup you proclaim the death of the Lord until He comes" (I Cor 11:26). (4) We *anticipate* the heavenly banquet of eternity through the *ritual meal* of Holy Communion.

If the Eucharist is to be an effective instrument in bringing about and maintaining an earthly union between the Lord and ourselves, these four major symbols of the Mass must be living symbols and not mere lifeless signs. Symbols become alive whenever the transcendent dimension of the corresponding functions is activated. The more fully we can activate this transcendent dimension, the more alive, meaningful, and grace-filled the Eucharistic celebration will be. Because different temperaments find it easier to activate the transcendent dimension of one function rather than another, a good Eucharistic celebration should endeavor to evoke the use of all four functions through the four basic symbols of the Eucharist. Otherwise, some persons in the congregation will not be reached and affected. A knowledge of human temperaments and some insight into the different ways to activate the transcendent dimension of each of the four psychological functions will help to accomplish this.

As the Eucharist is now constituted the main burden for a good experience of the presence of the Risen Lord falls upon the priest-celebrant. His task, therefore, is to see that the Eucharistic celebration and especially the homily satisfy the different spiritual needs of the four basic temperaments. The celebrant must be aware that different human temperaments are affected in different ways. In his homily he should make a special effort to say something that appeals to each of the four functions and the four basic temperaments. For instance, if his development is logical it will strike a resonant chord with those whose Dominant is Thinking; if his voice is pleasant and well-modulated, the Sensers will take notice more readily; if his sincerity and enthusiasm show, the Feelers and the Intuitives will respond to him. Furthermore, if theological concepts are presented, the NTs will be satisfied; while a hearkening back to tradition and the history of doctrinal development will alert the SJs to attention and interest. If comment is made on how the readings relate to one's life today, the NFs will be reached; whereas, if a dramatic action of self-denial or mission is called for, the SPs will emotionally and mentally respond.

With the emphasis of Vatican II on the ministry of lay persons and the formation of liturgy committees in parishes, more people can, and should, be taught how to assist the presider in making the liturgy a drama that will sweep one's being up into a fuller participation in the life of the Risen Lord. In any good theatrical or play production, preparation and adherence to detail must be done beforehand to set the stage properly. For the ritual of the Mass, the cast and crew (the laity) can help the director of the liturgy (the priest-celebrant) by creating a correct and beautiful setting (the altar appointments, the flowers, the lighting, the acoustics, and the sound) and by being prepared for participation by previous study of the Word to be proclaimed (pre-reading of the script, "the book of the play"). In preparation, also, in the form of advance notice and reviews, a liturgy committee can work to arouse a feeling of community so that when all congregate, the warmness of the group leads to the anticipation of a "good show", namely, a fine Christian celebration of the Eucharist. Thus, all functions and temperaments, represented in the congregation, will be involved; and they in turn will assure that the liturgy speaks to the other persons of the same temperament in the congregation.

The Feeling Function and the Community of Believers

The basic symbol present at the Eucharist is the community of baptized persons who accept Jesus Christ as their Lord and Savior and who believe in the power of his life, death, and resurrection to save them. Without a congregation of believers constituted of a celebrant or leader and at least one or more persons it is impossible to have a complete Eucharist. An ancient law of the Church specifies that a priest should not celebrate the Eucharist alone but only with a congregation. In the Gospel Jesus says, "Where there are two or more gathered in my name, there I am in the midst" (Matt 18:20). Belief in the presence of the Risen Lord in every gathering of Christian believers is an elemental symbol of Christianity that goes back to the first Pentecost.

The Feeling Function, which grasps the value of personhood, must operate in order to have an experience of community. The transcendent dimension of the Feeling Function must be activated in order for a Eucharistic congregation to experience and accept the presence of the living, Risen Lord in their spirit-filled community. Feeling or emotion is not sufficient to experience the real presence of Jesus Christ. Faith, which has made a value judgment, and grace, which is God's gift, must also be present; but faith and grace without the transcendent dimension of the relational Feeling Function will not engender community. Without a well-activated transcendent dimension of the Feeling Function, which relates to God as a person and to the presence of Christ in each believer, the symbol of community in Christ and in one another becomes a dead symbol. Hence, the necessity on the part of the celebrant, ministers, and congregation to prepare for the liturgy beforehand by developing an intimacy with the Lord during their personal prayer periods throughout the week. If everyone has worked hard to develop a relationship with Jesus Christ Our Lord during their daily personal prayer-time, the Eucharistic celebration will resound with the intense feeling of the assembled and become a tremendous experience of the presence of God. Through prior preparation, the sense of the presence of the Lord and a sense of community become very real and powerful during the Eucharistic celebrations of a vibrant retreat group or any other group which has shared in study and preparation. Even though the persons on retreat have previously been strangers to one another and are observing strict silence, a beautiful community experience nevertheless may be had each time the group gathers for Eucharist; and in that community celebration together they have a new and tremendous experience of the presence of the Lord Jesus Christ among them.

The key word to describe this experience of *community* is *celebration*. Wherever a group of spirit-filled Christians gather for Eucharist, a celebration of our oneness in faith occurs in that we all have heard and believe in the Good News of Jesus Christ. Even

Christian funeral masses become a celebration not of death but of our faith in resurrection. All the four basic temperaments and all sixteen personality types need and can enjoy the experience of a community celebration. Because the NF temperament usually has the most highly developed Feeling Function and understands best the value of personhood and community, the NF persons in the congregation have a special responsibility to see that this symbol of community remains alive and active, rather than lifeless and useless, during each liturgy. The SJ persons who have Feeling as either their Dominant or Auxiliary Function will be a great help to the NFs toward making the symbol of community alive and vibrant. Whereas, those SJ persons, whose Feeling Function is their Inferior or Tertiary Function, are like the NTs who need a community celebration in order to activate their dormant Feeling. Probably the SP persons need the experience of community most; so much so that, if this dimension of Eucharist is absent, the SPs soon vote with their feet and stop attending the Eucharist gathering.

Before Vatican II a great deal of the power of the Eucharistic symbol of community had been lost. For most Catholics the Mass was a private encounter with God. Many good Catholics had developed their own individual ways of making contact with God at Mass, and those who had succeeded best were the most upset with the liturgical reforms. Instead of allowing their private devotions to continue during Mass, the Church insisted that they experience the reality of a Christian community. Since the reforms of Vatican II we have had varying success in restoring new life to the Eucharistic symbol of community. There is still much resistance to it from many quarters and much work still to be done to make this symbol a living experience of the presence of the risen Lord Jesus Christ.

We are suggesting here that one of the best ways to make this symbol of community a living symbol is the activation. of the transcendent dimension of the Feeling Function, which should begin with the celebrant, include all those who assist in the Eucharistic celebration, and then reach out and embrace the whole congregation. However, to wait until Sunday morning to start activating one's Feeling Function is to wait too late. All week long during a daily prayer period the priest, ministers, and congregation need to concentrate on attaining an intimacy with God and a relational attitude toward others by bringing their Feeling Function into conscious expression.

The Thinking Function and the Word of God

After community, the next most obvious symbol present in the Eucharist is the comprehension of the Word of God in the Sacred Scriptures. Almost immediately after the community gathers for liturgy, the reading or proclamation of the Word takes place. Every word of the Sacred Scriptures is a symbol of the presence and power of God and God's truth upon earth; and when properly explained and understood, these words become a true experience of His living presence. Although the lectors and homilist have the primary responsibility to "break open" the Word of God so that it becomes fully intelligible to the assembled, the proclamation of the Word of God at liturgy requires the cooperation of everyone in the congregation. Each member of the community has a responsibility not only to listen attentively and intelligently but also to prepare for the liturgical proclamation of the Word by previous study of the Scriptures at home. Any member of the congregation who approaches the liturgical proclamation of the Word without prior preparation is doing a disservice not only to him/herself but also to the rest of the congregation.

The conscious use of the Thinking Function, as well as the activation of the transcendent dimension of the Thinking Function, are needed in order to make the Word of God alive and meaningful. The conscious dimension of the Thinking Function is activated through the study of Scripture commentaries, Bible history, and the other available source knowledge of the Bible; but the transcendent dimension of Thinking will open the door to the transcendental level of truth where God dwells and thus lead to a deeper, inner spiritual wisdom.

The Bible is called the Word of God because it is more than mere human words. It is a message from the transcendent God. Human words by their very nature are finite and limited, whereas God is infinite and unlimited. When God communicates with human beings, He adjusts Himself to our level and uses human language and terms. These human words of the Bible have a richer meaning than the obvious, literal, human sense. We need therefore to activate the transcendent dimension of our Thinking Function in order to interpret authentically the true meaning of God's Word. We speak of the need "to break open" the Scriptures in order to discern their deeper, spiritual meaning. To accomplish this, we need a combination of divine grace, faith, knowledge, and understanding through the activation of the transcendent dimension of all four functions but especially through that of Thinking and Intuition.

Therefore, it would be natural to expect that those with the NT temperament should make the greatest contribution to instilling new life into this second Eucharistic symbol, the Word. Actually, all the temperaments and all the functions have a part to play if the proclamation of the Word of God during the Eucharist is to become truly vibrant and speak to each member of the Christian community. St. Paul speaks of the Word of God as a two-edged sword which is able to convict, convince, convert, and sanctify. If the symbol of the Word is truly alive, abundant evidence of its power wll be seen in a visible experience of conversion and metanoia on the part of the congregation. In the history of Christianity we have had many experiences when the symbol of the Word was truly alive and converted thousands of persons: for instance through John and Samuel Wesley in England, St. Francis Xavier in India, Jonathan Edwards in this country, St. Francis of Assisi in Italy.

The Eucharistic symbol of the Word is present not only during the proclamation at the Liturgy of the Sacred Scriptures but also in all the other words used throughout the Eucharistic celebration — for instance, in the songs that are sung. All of us have experienced how grace-filled and meaningful a Eucharist can be when there is good and appropriate singing in which the congregation can participate. Also, our Catholic and Christian faith postulates that the words of the Eucharistic Prayer, especially the Words of Institution, when spoken with faith, have the power to make really and truly present the living Lord Jesus under the appearances of the bread and wine.

The key word to describe our reaction to the living symbol of the Word is *CONTEMPLATION* of divine Truth. Whenever the symbolism of the Word is truly alive, the whole Eucharistic congregation will find themselves "lost" in contemplation of the power and presence of the truth of the living God.

The Sensing Function and the Cross

From the very beginning of Christianity the Eucharist has been seen as proclaiming the Paschal Mystery of the death of Jesus on the cross. St. Paul, writing to the Corinthians a mere twenty or thirty years after the events of Good Friday, stated "Every time you eat this bread and drink this cup, you proclaim the death of the Lord until he comes" (I Cor 11:26). Catholic theology has defined the Mass as "the unbloody sacrifice of the Cross". In the Gospel Jesus uses the symbol of the Cross to express the path of non-violence which he choose to follow and which he insisted his disciples must also follow.

All the functions have a part to play to make and keep the symbol of the Cross a living force in the Eucharist. We need to **think** about the true meaning of the cross, and we need to activate our **Feeling Function** in order to identify with the sufferings of Jesus on the cross. Our **Intuition** will also help us understand the hidden Mystery of the Cross. However, the **Sensing Function** will be the most affected when we reflect deeply upon this symbol of the Cross and the Crucifixion. The outward sufferings connected with the crucifixion are meant to symbolize a whole new way of life introduced by Jesus Christ to resolve the problem of evil in the world. Sensers, who live in the present, in the here and now, are the types who are most prepared to incorporate this dimension of the Christ-life into their own life. Therefore, we all need to activate the transcendent dimension of our Sensing Function in order to appreciate the spiritual value of the Cross.

The symbol of the Cross is closely connected to another ancient symbol which is still very much present in the dreams of modern people as well as in the mythology of ancient peoples. Throughout history the symbol of the dragon has been used to express the powers of evil confronting mankind on earth. In the third chapter of Genesis, the forces of evil are represented by the serpent, which is but another, more devious, form of the ancient dragon.

Throughout the long history of paganism the recommended method for handling the dragon was to slay it; and we see a similar attitude toward evil throughout most of the pages of the Old Testament. The violence of evil was met by the violence of the sword, and thereby the power of evil was counteracted or neutralized for the time being. The most dramatic example of this method of handling the dragon of evil was the fierceness employed by Joshua and the Israelites when they entered Canaan. But, this method of "slaying the dragon" never proved to be permanently effective in eliminating evil and establishing peace. Invariably the dragon revived in the next generation and continued its opposition to good; and a new wave of violence was undertaken to neutralize the power of evil once again. This has been the constant experience of the human race in its struggles with the powers of evil on earth.

By his passion and death, through "the paradox of the cross", Jesus instituted a new way of conquering the dragon. In the goodness of his love, Jesus submitted himself to the dragon and allowed it to kill him. To all outward appearances the forces of evil conquered Jesus on Good Friday. The "dragon" seemed to have won an uncontested victory over the forces of good by putting the God-man to death. However, God's last word was not spoken on Good Friday but on Easter Sunday. The last word was not death on a cross but the new, glorious, immortal life of the Risen Lord. Thus, the symbol of the Cross was introduced into human history as God's ultimate answer for resolving the problem of evil on earth. Victimhood was presented to the world as the way of lasting peace. A new chapter was written in the ancient epic of the conquering of evil.

This new way of encountering and conquering "the dragon" was so revolutionary, so different from the traditional way of handling one's enemies and confronting evil, that only the first few generations of Christians really took it seriously. In the first 300 years Christian martyrs did practice victimhood, and the result was the conquest of paganism in both the West and the East. However, beginning with Constantine in the fourth century and continuing through the Middle Ages and modern times, we once again resorted to the pagan method of attempting to slay the dragon. Christians revived this ancient pagan myth in the legend of St. George and the dragon; and during the centuries of Christian knighthood the cross became a sword for slaying the enemies of Christianity. Holy wars were fought in the name of God and Jesus Christ; and theologians, beginning with St. Augustine, devised the conditions for conducting a just war. Most Christians soon took it for granted that the use of violence was justified in overcoming evil when all other methods failed. It became the patriotic duty of Christians to take up the sword in defense of their country and its rights.

The Cross was still mounted on church steeples and other religious buildings; and the Mass was still spoken of as the unbloody sacrifice of the cross; but for all practical purposes, and for most Christians, after the fourth century the Cross lost its symbolic meaning as God's way for handling the dragon of evil in the world. We still spoke of "taking up our cross and following Christ", but we used the symbol of the Cross merely to mean the sufferings, struggle, and pain which individual humans had to experience on earth in order to lead a good and Christ-like life. The symbolism of the Cross did not die out completely, but the meaning given to it by Jesus was greatly emasculated.

Amazingly, a non-Christian, Mahatma Gandhi, rediscovered the full symbolism of the Cross and re-introduced Jesus' teaching on victimhood into the modern world. The non-violent methods for overcoming evil practiced by Gandhi contain all the elements of authentic Christian victimhood. Gandhi had no hesitation in stating that his "Satagraha" (truth force) was based on the teachings and example of Jesus Christ. Following Gandhi's example, Martin Luther King, Jr. also used non-violence to vanquish the evil of racism in this country. Now, in the face of the terrible threat of a world-wide nuclear holocaust, victimhood is again being suggested as the Christian solution to a lasting world peace. Instead of trying to slay the dragon, we are challenged to convert the dragon by love, truth, goodness, and non-violence even at the price of our own death. We seem to have rediscovered the symbolism of the Cross as taught and practiced by Jesus on Calvary.

On the night before he died, Jesus gave to the Christian community a means, the Eucharist, to relive and proclaim the symbol of the Cross in every succeeding generation. If this third symbol can become alive and meaningful in our Eucharistic liturgies, we today would thereby receive the necessary grace, strength, and courage to take up our own cross and victimhood and follow this Christian way of conquering the dragon. However, for this to happen, the transcendent dimension of the four psychological functions needs to be activated and experienced during the Eucharist. We must look beyond the mere, outward, sensing appearances of Jesus' crucifixion and see the Cross as a symbol of agapic love whereby we, here and now, can overcome the evil of the world. By our Feeling Function we will activate the power to love our enemies as Jesus did and respect their dignity. We must activate the transcendent level of our Thinking Function to perceive the Cross as the reconciling symbol of truth which resolves the problem of evil. Through our Intuitive Function we can see the problem of evil from the expanded viewpoint of God rather than through our own human keyhole vision.

The key word to describe this third symbol, *the Cross*, is *commemoration*. More than a mere pious remembrance of Jesus' death, liturgical commemoration means "making present" once again the past event in order for the people of today to become a part of the never-ending experience of the Paschal Mystery of the Cross. An authentic celebration of the Eucharistic Liturgy enables us to experience anew the victimhood of Jesus on Calvary; and if this third symbol, the Cross, is truly alive, the participants in the liturgy receive the grace and psychic energy to offer themselves, after the example of Jesus, as victims of love to counteract the powers of evil in the world. The SJ persons in the congregation should be the first to understand, appreciate, and preserve this dimension of COMMEMORATION. Therefore, they have the main responsibility to help those of other temperaments experience the true meaning of the liturgical commemoration of the Cross. However, all the functions and all the temperaments have a contribution to make if we are to restore full life to the Eucharistic symbol of the Cross.

The Intuitive Function and the Ritual Meal

The fourth symbol of an authentic Eucharistic liturgy is the ritual meal which is meant to be an anticipation of the heavenly banquet to which we are invited after death. The first Eucharist celebrated by Jesus the night before he died was a ritual meal which we call the Lord's Supper. In using a ritual meal, Jesus followed two Jewish traditions which used the context of a sacred meal to express God's presence, friendship, and union with the chosen people. The first of these, the Passover Supper, celebrating God's continual protection and presence among them, has been a religious symbol for Jews and Israelites for more than three thousand years. At the time of Jesus' public ministry, the Jews also had another ritual, the Berakah, which consisted of the blessing of a loaf of bread at the beginning of a regular family meal and the distribution of a piece of the bread to each family member. At the end of the meal, a common cup of wine was blessed and shared by all those at table. In the blessing of the bread and wine, the head of the house recalled the whole history of God's salvation of His people. The Jews believed that, whenever they participated in the Berakah, they made the God of their ancestors really and truly present to work similar deeds for them.

Just as the Jews believed that they made Yahweh really and truly present to them through the ritual meal of Berakah and Passover, so most Christians have believed from the very beginning that the Eucharistic meal made the Risen Lord Jesus really and truly present to them. The first Christian communities acknowledged that the ritual meal of the Lord's Supper was actually a Christian Passover meal whereby believers in Christ could celebrate their delivery from the Angel of Death just as the Israelites were similarly delivered in Egypt through the Passover.

Therefore, a ritual meal of commemoration became the relational symbol through which the living presence of the Risen Lord was experienced at the gatherings of the early Christians. We are told that on the first Easter Sunday evening the two disciples at Emmaus recognized Jesus in the breaking of the bread. Down through the centuries the majority of Christians have continued to believe in the real presence of the Risen Christ under the appearances of the bread and wine at the Eucharistic meal. Unfortunately, much of the symbolism of a sacred banquet in our Eucharistic celebrations has been lost. A stranger would find it difficult to recognize the average Sunday Liturgy as a sacred banquet or meal. The only survival of this symbol of eating and drinking is at Holy Communion where more often than not the eating consists of a thin, round, white wafer placed on the tongue or in the hand of the communicant. In many parishes the congregation is still denied access to the cup. Even the most vivid and creative imagination has difficulty seeing this state of affairs as a heavenly banquet.

When Jesus instituted the Eucharist at the Last Supper he told his disciples: "I tell you I shall not drink again of this fruit of the vine until that day when I drink it new with you in my Father's kingdom" (Matt 26:29). In St. John's Gospel Jesus also speaks of this ritual meal as an anticipation of everlasting life: "He who eats my flesh and drinks my blood has everlasting life and I will raise him up at the last day. For my flesh is food indeed and my blood is drink indeed" (Jn 6:54-55).

Intuition, which is the future-looking faculty of the human psyche, is needed to appreciate this dimension of *ANTICIPATION* in the Eucharist. The Eucharistic meal is meant to be a foreshadowing of our eternal union with God and the Risen Lord Jesus in heaven. Just as the communion bread and wine of the Eucharist are incorporated within us when we eat and drink them, so intuitively and symbolically we should experience here now on earth through the Eucharistic meal something of that future heavenly union with Jesus. "The cup of blessing which we bless, is it not a participation in the blood of Christ? The bread which we break, is it not a participation in the body of Christ?" (I Cor 10:16).

By activating the transcendent dimension of the Intuitive Function, we should be able to experience each Eucharist as a return of the Risen Lord to earth to refresh and strengthen us with the food and drink of his own resurrected body and blood. Some Christians rebel at the idea of eating human flesh and drinking human blood. What they fail to realize is that we do not eat and drink physical flesh and blood but rather are united in a most intimate way with the resurrected body of the glorified Christ. Through divine grace and faith, the transcendent dimension of our Intuition grasps and accepts this. We are able to see each Eucharist as an experience similar to that described in the last chapter of St. John's Gospel where the Risen Lord returns to earth at the Sea of Tiberias. After directing the apostles where to cast their nets, he invites them to bring their boats ashore and serves them a meal of fish and bread. During the Liturgy of the Word, the Risen Lord returns to our midst in order to instruct us where "to cast our nets for a catch". Then in the ritual meal of bread and wine, Jesus refreshes and strengthens us for our journey in faith toward the kingdom of heaven. Through grace-filled Intuition we can have an experience of anticipation of the heavenly banquet of the future kingdom.

Thanks to the liturgical reforms of Vatican II we once again are able to experience the living symbols of Community and Word. Also our new understanding and acceptance of "victimhood" can bring new meaning to the symbol of the Cross. But, ways must be found to put new life into the symbol of the sacred meal. Besides Intuition, the other three functions — Sensing, Thinking, and Feeling — must be activated in their transcendent dimension to restore life to the nearly dead symbol of a ritual meal.

Since 75% of the average congregation have Sensing as their Dominant or Auxiliary Function, the first appeal should be to arouse the transcendent dimension of Sensing. For example, we can make more obvious the symbolism of the breaking of the bread before Holy Communion. Large hosts or larger loaves of Eucharistic bread might be used; and then these should be broken in full view of the congregation with a verbal recollection of St. Paul's statement to the Corinthians to vivify the communal meal aspect. "Because the loaf of bread is one, we, many though we are, are one body, for we all partake of the one loaf" (I Cor 10:17). Furthermore, people should be urged to partake sufficiently of the cup of consecrated wine rather than merely touching the cup to their lips. A pleasant-tasting wine should be chosen and an adequate quantity taken so that its sweetness and tingling warmth will be felt by the communicant. "Taste and see the sweetness (goodness) of the Lord."

The homilist at the Mass can activate the symbol-making dimension of the Thinking Function of members of the congregation by explaining the implications and tradition of a community meal. Once this is pointed out, everyone can recognize the symbolic meaning of sitting down to a meal with friends. To sit down at table and eat with another human being is universally recognized as a sign of friendship and an acceptance of our table-mates as equals. In the past, for this reason, many white Southerners refused to allow Blacks to eat at the same table or in the same room as they did. As a ritual meal, the Eucharist very clearly expresses the willingness and desire of Jesus Christ to be our friend and table-mate. Just as the Risen

Christ ate and drank with his apostles after the resurrection, so he continues to accept us as his friends at the Eucharistic table. He invites us to his table, and through the act of partaking in Holy Communion we are assured of a place at his heavenly banquet in heaven.

The Thinking Function also allows one to reflect upon the symbolism of the many grains of wheat crushed to be ground into flour and submitted to the oven's heat to be baked. We, though many members, also need to be ground into flour and baked in order to become the Body of Christ. As the many small grapes which are crushed and fermented to become the wine, we too must experience diminishment and suffering to join ourselves to our fellow human beings in order to become the one body of Christ.

During Eucharist the Feeling Function may also be activated in regard to the symbol of a meal by recalling a similar ritual which is used the world over to express hospitality. When a guest visits, the host is usually expected to offer something to drink and perhaps something to eat. This offering by the host and the acceptance by the guest is universally recognized as a symbol of hospitality and friendship. One would not make such an offer to someone, or accept it from someone, whom one considered an enemy. Furthermore, when a reconciliation is achieved between two former antagonists, the universal symbol to express this is by the two persons having a cup of coffee together, or having a drink together, or in some way sharing food and drink together. Similarly, the Eucharistic meal, with its partaking of the bread and cup, is a symbolic act which expresses God's love and friendship for us and our acceptance of this love and our reciprocation of friendship toward God. It is also meant to be a symbolic act expressing our intention to practice love and friendship toward our neighbor.

Conclusion

The fact that down through the centuries the Eucharist has continued to be a source of grace and a means of sanctification for countless persons is proof enough that the power of its symbols never has been lost completely. COMMUNITY, WORD, CROSS, and MEAL are always present in every valid celebration of Eucharist. However, a great deal of grace and psychic energy have been lost by the failure of modern persons to appreciate fully the meaning of these four symbols. The rediscovery of the power of symbols by modern depth psychology and the subsequent interest in them should help to revitalize our Eucharistic symbols. Quite interestingly, Carl G. Jung was so impressed with the power of the symbols of the Mass that he wrote a long treatise on *Transformation Symbolism in the Mass*.

Each of the four psychological functions and each of the four temperaments have a distinct contribution to make to modern liturgical renewal. The more proficient we can become in using the transcendent dimension of each of the functions during our personal prayer, the more we will be able to contribute to making the Sunday Liturgy a true experience of the presence and power of the living God and the Risen Lord Jesus Christ. Together, the four symbols of COMMUNITY, WORD, CROSS, and RITUAL MEAL can give us an experience of unity with God, with the Risen Jesus, and with the whole Communion of Saints, both living and dead.

EPILOGUE

As stated in the Introduction "everything said in this book about the relationship of temperament and prayer should be taken with certain reservations." Our recommendations will not apply to everyone since each of us is a unique person with our own particular background of experience. However, since so many people have benefited from the suggestions found herein, the authors feel justified in presenting their findings and conclusions to a wider audience. Moreover, the great interest aroused by our Prayer Project of 1982 indicated the need of assembling under one cover the various papers we have written. Requests for more information on the topic arrive from far and near almost every day. Therefore in view of this demand and the almost complete absence of published material on the subject, we felt called to publish this present book.

Our hope is that this book will stir up even more interest in the subject so that many others will proceed along this thesis and make further contributions to it. The hunger and thirst for more knowledge concerning spirituality, prayer, and their relationship to personality type and psychological functioning can be satisfied only if many others apply their wisdom and experience to the subject. We would appreciate any comments, criticisms, and contributions on the topic which the reader would be willing to share with us. We are especially anxious to receive comments on the worthwhileness of the prayer suggestions which we give in Chapters Three to Seven. You may send any such material to THE OPEN DOOR, INC., P. O. Box 855, Charlottesville, Virginia 22902.

A word of caution must be given about the consequences of following exclusively any one of the types of prayer or spirituality described. *Lectio Divina*, if used without being balanced by virtual prayer of action, could result in too much introspection. Ignatian spirituality must be on its guard against Phariseeism or Externalism which was so thoroughly condemned by Jesus in the Gospels. "These people honor me with their lips but their hearts are far from me" (Mt 15:8). For Franciscan spirituality, the heresy of "good works" or Pelagianism is the extreme against which one must be on guard. The free spirit must practice self-discipline and spend some formal time with God each day. Otherwise, good works will degenerate into mere secularistic humanism, the prevailing religion of the majority of Americans today. Augustinian spirituality must beware of the heresy, Manicheanism, to which Augustine himself fell victim. We may become so engrossed in the things of the spirit that we begin to neglect the body and to think of the things of the flesh as evil. "And God saw everything that He had made and behold it was very good" (Gen 1:31). Thomistic spirituality is apt to be a very intense form of spirituality and can fall victim to Jansenism which grossly exaggerates the requirements needed for salvation, thus denying heaven to a major portion of the general population. Religion and prayer then become an elitist movement which is only for those who follow all the obligations which the NT architects of sanctity dream up in their speculations. We know that Jansenism among Catholics and Puritanism among Protestants are two heresies that indeed have done great harm to the religious life of our people. There is always this danger of carrying something good to the extreme of fanaticism, thus making it no longer totally beneficial but potentially harmful.

We are firmly convinced from our experience in working with the various personality types that the suggestions given in this book will strike a responsive chord with the majority of you. Try them, use them for a while, experiment with the different types of prayer until you discover for yourself the type or types of prayer best suited to your personality. But, please do not allow yourself to become stifled with just one type of prayer. Enjoy the riches of all the different kinds of prayer by, at least occasionally, making the effort to practice those forms of prayer which require extra psychic energy and effort on your part. Your pains will be handsomely rewarded.

APPENDIX I

DISCOVERING YOUR TYPE

The following outline of the qualities of the basic attitudes and functions will be helpful to those who do not have access to the Myers Briggs Type Indicator (MBTI) and perhaps also to those who have already been exposed to this instrument of personality determination and whose scores have been borderline or in question. At any rate, our hope is that through this summary you will get a better understanding of the underlying characteristics behind these personality attributes. We recommend that, if at all possible, the reader take the MBTI to determine by this prescribed method one's type from among the sixteen personality types.

In making your decision as to which four of the eight groups apply to you, read the descriptions of both sections of each pair of the preferences as described below and find the side that most nearly fits your usual way of acting. All of us have some facility in all eight areas, but we tend to prefer one side of each of the four pairs. You should always finish with one letter from each of the four pairs of preferences to complete your personality type. There are sixteen possible combinations of the eight letters: ESTJ, ESTP, ISTJ, ISTP, ESFJ, ESFP, ISFJ, ISFP, ENTJ, INTJ, ENTP, INTP, ENFJ, ENFP, INFJ, INFP.

To determine to which of the four basic temperaments (NT, NF, SP, SJ) you belong, take the *second* letter of your four-letter personality type, which will be either an S or an N. If it is an S, then take the *fourth* letter of your personality, which will be either a J or a P. Thus, you will have two letters, either SJ or SP. If your second letter is an N, take the *third* letter of your personality type, which will be either a T or an F. Again you will have two letters, either NF or NT. These then constitute the four basic temperaments: SJ (Ignatian), SP (Franciscan), NT (Thomistic), and NF (Augustinian).

EXTRAVERTS

-are primarily interested in the outer world, oriented toward other people and other's reactions to what one does or says

-like to have people around them

-usually have many friends and acquaintancs

-plunge readily into new experiences

-get energy and stimulation from external things

-under stress need contact with other people

-in solving an issue say, "let's brainstorm"

-become bored when alone

-like variety and action

-are quite sociable, good mixers, good greeters

-usually introduce themselves first, seldom meet a stranger

-are concerned about what others say and think about them

-give their personal history and even ancestral history the first time you meet them

-prefer to speak rather than write, slow to answer letters but first to answer the phone

-show their Dominant Function to the world, easy to get to know

-are great conversationalists

INTROVERTS

-are primarily interested in the inner world of the spirit and their own reaction to people

-need time alone, are exhausted after a day of meeting people

-are not good salesmen unless deeply convinced of the value of product to be sold

-like to pause and take a sounding before plunging into anything new, distrust first impressions

-tend to be introspective and subjective

-prefer to work quietly and alone, are easily distracted by presence of other people

-feel very lonely in a crowd of strangers

-keep their inner life private and hidden except when with their closest friends

-show their Auxiliary Function to the world and reserve their Dominant Function for their inner life

-are independent of the outward situation, prefer to follow their own inner conscience

-under stress seek to get away by themselves

-when solving an issue say, "let's sleep on it"

-in conversation usually talk about other things rather than about themselves

SENSING TYPES

-are primarily concerned with the actual and the factual

-are good at judging the here and now situation

-have a practical eye for detail, have a photographic memory

-are good at giving directions

-value commonsense highly, are practical and realists

-want facts, trust facts, remember facts

-are down-to-earth persons, earth-bound, anchored to earth

-do not trust hunches until submitted to their practical commonsense and experience

-find it difficult to understand abstractions and symbols

-prefer and trust experience rather than hunches

-become impatient with complicated situations

-usually read the fine print of contracts

-are good at precise work, seldom make errors of fact or details

-find self-denial of senses difficult, are reluctant to sacrifice present enjoyment for future good

-need sense enjoyment, have high appreciation of sensual pleasures

INTUITIVE TYPES

-are more interested in future possibilities and potentials than in actual realities

-are always looking for some way to improve the present situation

-face life expectantly and will ski jump from the known to the unknown without filling in the gaps

-prefer to look at the whole picture and thus often overlook minor details

-are not good at giving directions

-are interested in the unknown and the complicated

-look for the inner meaning behind the facts and seek patterns in perceived facts

-are always looking around the corner to see what is ahead

-love to speculate about future possibilities and anticipate future events

-have frequent hunches, inspirations, insights that come "from out of the blue"

-are imaginative, original, creative, innovative

-dislike routine, prefer to learn a new skill

-work in bursts of energy and enthusiasm

-love myths, dreams, symbols, metaphors, visions

THINKING TYPES

-make judgments and decisions on an objective basis

-are ruled by their head rather than heart

-are rational, logical, straight-forward

-are ruled by principles, "the law and evidence"

-value logic more than sentiment

-are quite skillful in handling objective facts and ideas

-are very much concerned about justice, rights, reform, consistency in policy

-need to be treated fairly and justly

-are very good in executive and administrative positions

-love to discuss and argue, try to get to the bottom of every issue

-are good at argumentation and not excessively disturbed by conflict

-love to win at games of competition

-do not show feelings easily

-are uncomfortable in dealing with others' feelings and emotions

-find it difficult to handle praise

-are able to criticize, reprimand, and fire others without losing sleep over it

-tend to be impersonal and sometimes hurt others' feelings without realizing it

FEELING TYPES

-make decisions based on personal values and then try to find a logical reason to back these decisions

-are keenly aware of others' feelings

-are usually quite skillful and tactful in handling personal situations

-dislike telling people unpleasant things

-are ruled by the heart and feelings rather than by the head or logic

-are warm-hearted, forgiving, sentimental, capable of very deep feelings

-try to avoid conflict and therefore are usually good at resolving conflicts

-are concerned more about people than facts

-need praise and affirmation

-become deeply hurt when ignored, passed over, forgotten

-are good at enlisting volunteers and financial support for a cause that concerns the welfare of people

-enjoy work in counselling, ministry, social service or any position where there is an interaction with people who need to be helped

-often make decisions based on their own or others' personal likes and dislikes

JUDGING TYPES

-like things settled, finished as soon as possible, brought to closure

-live a planned, orderly life; prefer structure; dislike having to "fly by the seat of their pants"

-enjoy following a schedule and meeting a deadline

-like to know ahead of time to permit planning

-usually have a definite system for doing everything and are consistent in following it

-usually are prompt and on time for everything

-dislike last minute jobs

-dislike long shopping trips, prefer to go and buy the first thing that fits needs

-have a strong sense of accomplishment when finished with a task

-are active, decisive, able to get things done, "let's get this show on the road"

-are task-oriented, follow "management by objective"

-have a tendency to impose their will on others and try to control the world in which they live.

-try to put everyone on schedule — usually their schedule

-can be rigid since they usually have a settled opinion and position on most things

PERCEIVING TYPES

-are flexible, open-minded; continually try to discover more data

-are reluctant to make final decisions

-frequently wait until the last minute to make a decision

-may postpone unpleasant jobs, "wait and see"

-dislike deadlines

-feel cramped by a tight schedule

-live life in a spontaneous, free-spirited manner

-are crisis-oriented, ready to go in any direction in an emergency

-have the best in them brought out by emergencies and crises

-like to leave things flexible, unsettled, so that they can make last minute alterations

-enjoy the unexpected, love surprises

-love to window-shop and find it difficult to buy until they have seen everything available

-make resolutions but seldom keep them

-are slow in answering mail that requires irrevocable decisions

-amass an astonishing store of information on any number of varied subjects

-are always receptive to new facts and allow the world to influence them

Now try to decide which side of each pair of preferences sums up your style of life. Your four letters should consist of one selection from each of the four pairs of preferences:

(E) Extravert—(I) Introvert
(S) Sensing——(N) Intuitive
(T) Thinking—(F) Feeling
(J) Judging——(P) Perceiving

This is your personality type. If you find yourself unable to choose one side of any of the four pairs of perferences, the likelihood is that you fit into the right side of the table: i.e., either Introvert, Intuitive, Feeling, Perceiving Types.

In this country our social, educational, industrial, military, and governmental way of life is somewhat biased to the left side of this personality scale, i.e., Extravert, Sensing, Thinking, Judging Types. Therefore, if on the MBTI you score in the middle or if you had difficulty in making a decision as to where you fit in the above suggested attributes, the likelihood is that your innate choice or preference is on the right side of the scale. After many years of research and consideration, Isabel Briggs Myers arrived at this conclusion. Her rational was that those on the right side of the scale are forced to swim against the current of public approbation or acceptance, and so if one finds oneself caught in the middle, then the likelihood is that by nature we are inclined to the right side. This conclusion has proved to be accurate in most situations where a person has difficulty deciding which side of a pair of preferences to choose.

Appendix II

Prayer Suggestions for the Sixteen Individual Types

THE PRAYER OF THE ESTP TYPE
(Basic Temperament = SP)

DOMINANT-Sensation, AUXILIARY-Thinking
INFERIOR-Intuition, TERTIARY-Feeling

ESTPs are people of action, unpredictable, yet resourceful promoters, pragmatists. They in truth can say that their work is their prayer provided it is done for the glory of God and the welfare of their neighbor.

ESTPs do not need as much formal prayer as other types; but if their work is to be put in the right perspective, they must have a sincere and moral commitment to truth, to justice, to charity, and to the recognition of the personal value of others. Frequently it is difficult for this type to make a deep commitment, so this is the area in which they need to concentrate. Otherwise, they will make a god out of their own desires and ambitions for power. ESTPs often find it difficult to live under tension and so try to avoid stress at all costs, even by flight to some other place or concern. To overcome this temptation, they need a practical regime of regular self-discipline and self-sacrifice.

Besides praying while working, driving, etc., the ESTP needs at least a half hour of formal prayer and meditation each day. The *Lectio Divina* of St. Benedict would be the recommended form this daily prayer might take. This means spending a few minutes reading a passage of Sacred Scripture until a verse or short passage is found to speak to one's needs. Then perhaps ten or fifteen minutes should be spent in reflection on this passage in order to make application to oneself and to discover what God is trying to reveal. "What message is the Lord sending me?" "What is the Lord asking me to do?" "What change in my life is the Lord asking of me?" "What response should I make to the Word of the Lord?" The reflection should be the heart of the prayer period and should be followed by prayers of humility, contrition, gratitude, generosity, petition, praise, resolution, etc. as called for by the situation. Finally, at the end one should spend a few minutes to glorify and thank God for revealing His Word; then just be quiet and rest for a while in God's presence.

Centering Prayer, as taught by Father Basil Pennington, is another wonderful aid to the prayer-life of the ESTP. However, over the long haul, Franciscan types of prayer are apt to be the "bread and butter" prayers for most ESTPs. Spontaneous prayers and songs of praise and gratitude should be liberally sprinkled throughout the ESTP's day in order to help maintain a close union with God even in the midst of a busy work-day. When alone, prayers and songs may be recited or sung aloud.

Good experiences of community are essential to the spiritual growth of the ESTP and are normally found at Sunday Mass. However, if this is lacking, these experiences might be found elsewhere, for example, in a prayer group. ESTPs desire and need to share their faith journey with others and have others share their faith journey with them. The Cursillo Movement can provide the ESTP with experiences of Christian community during the original Weekend as well as in Team Formation, Group Reunion, and Monthly Ultreya. ESTPs usually enjoy singing and giving praise to God. It is important to practice this in a good Christian community setting.

Spiritual experiences of the ESTPs are usually concerned with the details of their own life, such as dramatic answers to personal prayers. They are frequently able to experience the presence of God, the love of God, and the protection of God. Some ESTPs also experience ESP (Extra Sensory Perception) and deep, intuitive knowledge of persons and events even at a distance.

The Books of the Bible that are attractive to the ESTP are the Canticles of Praise in the Old Testament (e.g. Daniel 3:26-90), Psalms of Praise, Gospel of John, and the Gospel of Mark with its action-oriented description of the life of Jesus.

Developing and Recognizing
The Potential of the ESTP Shadow

Become familiar with the basic attributes of the INFJ personality, which is your opposite in type. Consider how you do not use your Inferior Function of Intuition and Tertiary Function of Feeling to the fullest. When reading the portrait of the INFJ type, what specifically struck you as so different from your customary way of acting and doing? During your period of prayer think about how these new attributes and ways of relating could be manifested in your daily living. Meditate prayerfully on each one of the qualities of the INFJ that you wish to acquire by using perhaps the Thomistic method of prayerful consideration, asking yourself the questions: what, why, how, when, where, who, with what helps?

The shadow qualities that the ESTP should consider at prayer, ponder upon, and act upon are reflected in some or all of the following suggestions.

(1) Practice more depth of concentration when considering each situation in life.

(2) Become aware of your own feelings; express them through warmth, understanding, compassion, sympathy.

(3) Be sensitive to the needs and feelings of others; try to overcome selfish tendencies and be considerate of the needs of others.

(4) Show as much warmth as possible in relationships with others.

(5) Learn to base decisions on personal value as well as on logic.

(6) Look beyond the facts at hand and consider possiblities and future potential.

(7) Learn to live with tension and anxiety by deepening your trust in God and God's loving care.

(8) Plan, organize, and carry through to completion a major project.

(9) Be careful to complete a project that you have begun by personally taking care of the follow-up details and not by leaving them to someone else.

(10) Be faithful to commitments and relationships.

(11) Be a good listener, and do not pretend to know all that needs to be known.

(12) Learn to enjoy being alone at times.

THE PRAYER OF THE ISTP TYPE
(Basic Temperament = SP)

DOMINANT-Thinking, AUXILIARY-Sensation
INFERIOR-Feeling, TERTIARY-Intuition

ISTPs are very practical, precise, efficient, quiet, reserved, objective, factual. They are the artisans and craftsmen. They are good at exploration and usually possess tireless energy in pursuing the object of their search.

ISTPs prefer action over prayer and so will need to find ways of prayer that can be used while working. The Prayer of the Practice of the Presence of God (remembering that God is with us always) and the Jesus Prayer would be appropriate for this type. We recommend Brother Lawrence's book, *Practice of the Presence of God*, as a good book for study. It will help one to experience God in all the ordinary events of daily life.

Since they thrive on deep thinking and concentration, ISTPs need to spend at least thirty minutes daily in the practice of formal prayer. This may consist simply of just being silent and being with the Lord. In fact, ISTPs often prefer the silent liturgy of the weekday Mass. They need orderly structure as well as self-discipline in order to profit most from both public and private prayer.

They must remember that spiritual experiences will also be found in the presence of a spirit-filled community such as a Cursillo or some other group with which the ISTP feels comfortable and completely at home. ISTPs also need appreciation and understanding from others and therefore need at least a trustworthy spiritual friend and companion if not a larger group of like-minded friends with whom one can share. ISTPs will benefit from belonging to a prayer group only if it is well conducted, orderly, and has good spiritual sharing.

The *Lectio Divina* of St. Benedict, Franciscan prayer, and the Spiritual Exercises of St. Ignatius are appropriate prayer forms for use during the formal prayer periods. ISTPs might use their sensible imagination to place themselves in the scenes of the Gospel, as St. Ignatius recommends, but at the end they always should try to draw some practical fruit from their meditation.

If the *Lectio Divina* is used, half of the prayer period should be spent in meditating on the meaning of the Scripture passage or spiritual reading. Probably only about five minutes should be spent in the actual reading at the beginning of the period. One should read just long enough to get some worthwhile thought upon which one should then dwell for the next fifteen minutes. This should be followed by prayers of petition, humility, contrition, gratitude, resolution, commitment. Finally, a few quiet minutes should be taken before concluding to allow the new thoughts to sink more deeply into one's consciousness.

The Franciscan type of prayer is especially appealing to ISTPs. A suggestion for prayer is to imagine Jesus accompanying one on a walk in the country, or in a park, or around a lake, or by the ocean. "What might I say to Jesus and what might Jesus say to me?" The exchange should be totally free and spontaneous; this sort of setting and dialogue is especially appealing to the ISTPs.

ISTPs should feel free to try new and different ways of prayer and not become stuck in one form or method. In order to activate their Inferior Function of Feeling and their Tertiary Function of Intuition, Augustinian and Thomistic prayer forms should be used at least once a week. The more difficult type of prayer will be the Augustinian. The more simple the structure of their prayer, the more the ISTPs will benefit from it. ISTPs must learn to trust God to take care of things.

Recognizing and Developing
The Potential of the ISTP Shadow

Become familiar with the basic attributes of the ENFJ personality, which is your opposite in type. Consider how you do not use your Inferior Function of Feeling and your Tertiary Function of Intuition to the fullest. When reading the portrait of the ENFJ type, what specifically struck you as so different from your customary way of acting and doing? During your period of prayer think about how these new attributes and ways of relating could be manifested in your daily living. Meditate prayerfully on each one of the qualities of the ENFJ that you wish to acquire by using perhaps the Thomistic method of prayerful consideration, asking yourself the questions: what, why, how, when, where, who, with what helps?

The shadow qualities that the ISTP should consider at prayer, ponder upon, and act upon are reflected in some or all of the following suggestions.

(1) Show warmth and sympathy for others; be friendly, tactful; develop the feeling side of your personality and learn to express feelings openly before others.

(2) Develop some close friendships and spend prime time each week with them.

(3) Feel responsible for others.

(4) Be faithful to promises and commitments.

(5) Be cooperative even though you do not feel like it or see no value to it.

(6) Try to see the value of the opinion of the other with whom you disagree; in a discussion mention points of agreement before plunging into points of disagreement.

(7) Be tolerant of those with whom you disagree.

(8) Be open to hunches, inspirations, insights, possibilities. Follow and explore some of them. Look for the potential good behind obvious facts.

(9) Be willing to follow the rules and regulations at work or elsewhere, even though they seem unnecessary but are what others desire.

(10) Work to create harmony at home, in the work-place, community.

(11) Volunteer to be a leader of some committee or group.

(12) Take time to prepare for some event, action, project; and then follow it through to the end.

(13) Make a schedule for next week and stick to it.

(14) Resume some routines that have been neglected.

THE PRAYER OF THE ESTJ TYPE
(Basic Temperament = SJ)

DOMINANT-Thinking, AUXILIARY-Sensation
INFERIOR-Feeling, TERTIARY-Intuition

ESTJs are responsible, orderly, realistic, matter-of-fact, conservative, consistent. The ESTJs like Standard Operating Procedures and seek to preserve the established order. In their prayer life they may prefer traditional prayers such as the Divine Office. However, they may find the Rosary difficult since they are unable to do two things at once: meditate on the Mystery and say the prayers. They may also become easily distracted with the monotonous repetition. Therefore, they should attempt to be more spontaneous and conversational during the time of private prayer.

For liturgy, ESTJs prefer one that does not constantly change; and so many find it difficult to adjust to the frequent changes since Vatican II. Basically practical, law-and-order people, they will nevertheless follow the rules of the Church and be loyal to authority, even when interiorly they do not agree. ESTJs desire above all else to preserve the established order and keep the establishment healthy and balanced. They will resist any abrupt changes especially when they do not come from the properly constituted authority.

The ESTJ needs to spend a minimum of thirty minutes each day praying alone. During this period they should try spontaneous prayer from the heart in addition to using words composed by someone else. The Spiritual Exercises of St. Ignatius could be of great help to the growth of their spiritual life. ESTJs should train themselves to use their sensible imagination to project themselves back into the Gospel scenes and imagine what Jesus might say to them and what they in turn might say to Jesus. As St. Ignatius recommends, they should strive to draw from these contemplations of the events in the life of Jesus some fruit to use in their own life.

The Thomistic method of logical consideration and meditation on virtues and faults may also be a useful form of prayer for the ESTJ. With its orderly progression from spiritual reading to meditation, prayer, and contemplation, the Benedictine *Lectio Divina* will appeal to the ESTJ.

ESTJs may find belonging to a prayer group helpful because of the sharing and support given and received. As extraverts they need the support of others to maintain a good prayer life and continual growth on their spiritual journey. Similarly, they need good experiences of community and congregational participation at Sunday liturgy for the Eucharist to be truly meaningful.

That every ESTJ have the experience of a Cursillo Weekend and participate later on a Cursillo Team is highly recommended. The community spiritual experiences of prayer during a Cursillo Weekend, especially the daily Eucharist, should be a rich source of spiritual growth for the ESTJ.

If ESTJs will take the time to pray each day, they may expect deep comfort, support, help, and a sense of resting in the loving care of God, which will result in an inner peace and a feeling of closeness to God. Such experiences may happen very suddenly but rarely in the course of life; but the comfort and strength received from these moments of grace will enable the ESTJ to persevere along the path to holiness and salvation. ESTJs should strive to keep themselves open to the presence of the Holy Spirit and be ever willing to change the direction of their life in order to bring it more into conformity with the will of God.

Augustinian prayer will probably be the most difficult for the ESTJ since it requires the use of their Inferior and Tertiary Functions, but it is highly recommended that they use this type of prayer at least once a week. Franciscan prayer forms may not seem real prayers to them, but if used they too will prove of great spiritual benefit .

Recognizing and Developing The Potential of the ESTJ Shadow

Become familiar with the basic attributes of the INFP personality, which is your opposite in type. Consider how you do not use your Inferior Function of Feeling and your Tertiary Function of Intuition to the fullest. When reading the portrait of the INFP type, what specifically struck you as so different from your customary way of acting and doing? During your period of prayer think about how these new attributes and ways of relating could be manifested in your daily living. Meditate prayerfully on each one of the qualities of the INFP that you wish to acquire by using perhaps the Thomistic method of prayerful consideration, asking yourself the questions: what, why, how, when, where, who, with what helps?

The shadow qualities that the ESTJ should consider at prayer, ponder upon, and act upon are reflected in some or all of the following.

(1) Follow feelings, impulses, hunches rather than logic and reasoning.

(2) Find joy in pleasing others; be sensitive to the feelings of others.

(3) Show appreciation for other's merits; praise, compliment, affirm others; refer more often to what is well done than to what needs correction.

(4) Develop and express your feelings to others, especially to your family, spouse, and children.

(5) Show enthusiasm, warmth, sympathy for others.

(6) Do not jump to conclusions about others.

(7) Reserve judgment and avoid hasty judgments.

(8) Listen to other people's point of view, especially of those who ordinarily are not in a position to talk back.

(9) Show patience with those who do not carry out all details of a project.

(10) Study some topic for which you see no practical use but which you undertake just for the sake of learning.

(11) Look for possibilities and undeveloped potential for good.

(12) Keep one day a week unstructured, unplanned, open-ended. Go for a trip, or take off a day or afternoon, without having any previously made plans for its organization.

(13) Be open to ways and points of view other than your own.

(14) Be willing to deviate from Standard Operating Procedures.

(15) Be a follower sometimes and do what others want rather than what you want.

THE PRAYER OF THE ISTJ TYPE
(Basic Temperament = SJ)

DOMINANT-Sensation, AUXILIARY-Thinking
INFERIOR-Intuition, TERTIARY-Feeling

ISTJs are serious, quiet, thorough, orderly, logical, matter-of-fact. They are duty-oriented and no-nonsense persons who like everything organized, proper, straight-forward. They are the guardians of time-honored institutions, resistant to change, and conservative by nature. They find it difficult to handle strong feelings and emotions and so may give the impression of having ice in their veins when a decision has to be made. They can be pillars of strength for any institution and, with their strong convictions, can be charismatic leaders. Pope John Paul II is an ISTJ type.

Being introverted, the ISTJ needs to spend substantial time alone with God each day. Since St. Ignatius was an ISTJ, it would seem the Spiritual Exercises should be appropriate and appealing to the ISTJ temperament. The ISTJ must make an effort to develop the sensible imagination in order to project oneself back into the scenes of the Scripture as participant. For, example, St. Ignatius suggests that one should imagine oneself to be a servant boy or girl, present in the stable at the birth of Jesus, allowed to hold the Baby Jesus and listen to the conversation between Mary and Joseph and the Shepherds. Ignatius always ends each of his meditations with the advice: "And draw some practical fruit from the contemplation."

The *Lectio Divina* of St. Benedict, with its progression from spiritual reading, to meditation, oration, and finally contemplation, will also provide an orderly format for the prayer of the ISTJ. The Books of the Bible especially useful to the ISTJ would be the Gospel of St. Matthew, Isaiah, Acts, Psalms, Exodus, Numbers, and Deuteronomy. There is a great need for the ISTJ to learn the technique and develop the "art of listening" to God through the Scriptures or otherwise. Therefore, a Directed Retreat using the Spiritual Exercises might be very helpful as a means to learn and develop this practice of listening to God.

In order to activate the transcendent dimension of their Inferior and Tertiary Functions, the ISTJs should try to use Augustinian prayer at least once a week. This will help to develop their Feeling and Intuition Functions which otherwise will remain repressed and undifferentiated. Thomistic and Franciscan prayer forms should come somewhat easier to them and should also be used at least once weekly.

Because of their structure, both the Divine Office and the Rosary may be found helpful. The ISTJ may like set formulae of prayer but may feel the need to change them every few months or oftener in order to prevent routine from destroying one's union with God.

The ISTJs find great fulfillment in praying alone, but their highlighted prayer experiences will usually come through community or congregational experiences. Therefore, they may or may not find help in a Prayer Group. However, a Cursillo Weekend is strongly recommended for the ISTJ who may then find a small group reunion of like-minded friends with whom to meet and pray and reflect on a weekly basis. The ISTJ needs the support of a vibrant and faith-filled Christian community.

Since they usually find it difficult to express their feelings and to grasp or describe any deep spiritual experiences, it may be well for ISTJs to try keeping a Spiritual Journal. Writing in a journal would further the development of two faculties: their basic orderliness and their need for recall of their progression in the spiritual life.

The ISTJ can expect a sense of satisfaction that comes from conscientiously doing the will of God as revealed through one's conscience. Among the faith experiences that may come to the ISTJ will be: experiences of God's loving care and support as a clear answer to prayer, experiences of contrition for past sins and God's loving forgiveness, experiences of conversion and change in one's spiritual life.

Recognizing and Developing
The Potential of the ISTJ Shadow

Become familiar with the basic attributes of the ENFP personality, which is your opposite in type. Consider how you do not use your Inferior Function of Intuition and Tertiary Function of Feeling to the fullest. When reading the portrait of the ENFP type, what specifically struck you as so different from your customary way of acting and doing? During your period of prayer think about how these new attributes and ways of relating could be manifested in your daily living. Meditate prayerfully on each one of the qualities of the ENFP that you wish to acquire by using perhaps the Thomistic method of prayerful consideration, asking yourself the questions: what, why, how, when, where, who, with what helps?

The shadow qualities that the ISTJ should consider at prayer, ponder upon, and act upon are reflected in some or all of the following suggestions.

(1) Act occasionally on impulse.

(2) Look for new ways of doing things rather than the old, accustomed ways.

(3) Be open to future potential and possibilities.

(4) Try to develop a greater breadth of interest.

(5) Take extra pains to understand others and appreciate them.

(6) Make a special effort to relate to others.

(7) Be generous in giving thanks, praise, compliments, appreciation, affirmation to other people.

(8) Practice patience with others who do not see things as you do or who are not dependable.

(9) Show more warmth, feeling, understanding, consideration for the feelings of others.

(10) Make a deliberate attempt to be talkative without the help of alcohol when at some gathering of people.

(11) Be warmly enthusiastic about something.

(12) Take a day or afternoon off without planning anything ahead of time.

THE PRAYER OF THE ESFP TYPE
(Basic Temperament = SP)

DOMINANT-Sensation, AUXILIARY-Feeling
INFERIOR-Intuition, TERTIARY-Thinking

ESFPs are born leaders, good entertainers, very attractive personalities, and easily attract a large following. People enjoy having them around. Wherever they go, they bring warmth, excitement, optimism. ESFPs are the life of the party and love excitement. They are impulsive, frequently putting their foot in the wrong place.

The important thing for this temperament is to be with people and to be a part of the action. ESFPs will find a Prayer Group enjoyable because of the companionship and encouragement of the group. ESFPs will enjoy a Cursillo Weekend and add much to its success. They are generous and willing to accept people and things as they are and make the best of them. They love to be of service to others and are capable of the grand gesture of generosity, be it for God or for their fellow human beings.

ESFPs will probably find the externals of religion a help to their spiritual growth: lighted candles, crucifixes, sacred pictures, statues, incense, etc. They may be rather impulsive in their spiritual life, doing things and making gestures like long fasts and all night vigils. Dramatic Franciscan type of prayers will usually be their preferred form of prayer along with spontaneous prayers of praise and gratitude.

It is important, however, that ESFPs should also find time each day to pray alone and make contact with God. A half-hour daily should be spent speaking and listening to God. The *Lectio Divina* of St. Benedict should be especially appropriate for this type. Begin with spiritual reading of the Bible or some other book on matters religious, then meditate and reflect on its meaning, search for an application to oneself of what has been read — then, close with thanksgiving for the insights received, resolution of amendment, and some quiet time to bask in the goodness, love, glory, and beauty of God.

ESFPs are able to identify with the Passion of Christ quite well and therefore may find the Sorrowful Mysteries of the Rosary helpful. They are extremely generous in their willingness to sacrifice themselves for others. The Canticles of Praise scattered throughout the Old Testament, especially the Canticle of the Three Hebrew Youths in the fiery furnace (Daniel 3:26-90), will probably strike a responsive chord in their hearts. St. Francis' Canticle of the Sun and other similar prayers of praise of God's creation are most rewarding prayers for the ESFP temperament. The temperament of St. Francis of Assisi was probably ESFP.

ESFPs often experience God through direct, dramatic answers to their prayers of intercession. They also, like St. Francis, feel and experience God in nature, especially the animate nature of plants and animals. It is very much to their advantage to practice the needed discipline of exposing themselves to all the other types of prayer: Thomistic, Augustinian, and Ignatian.

Recognizing and Developing
The Potential of the ESFP Shadow

Become familiar with the basic attributes of the INTJ personality, which is your opposite in type. Consider how you do not use your Inferior Function of Intuition and your Tertiary Function of

Thinking to the fullest. When reading the portrait of the INTJ, what specifically struck you as so different from your customary way of acting and doing? During your period of prayer think about how these new attributes and ways of relating could be manifested in your daily living. Meditate prayerfully on each of the qualities of the INTJ that you wish to acquire by using perhaps the Thomistic method of prayerful consideration, asking yourself the questions: what, why, how, when, where, who, with what helps?

The shadow qualities that the ESFP should consider at prayer, ponder upon, and act upon are reflected in some or all of the following suggestions.

(1) Learn to trust intuitions, hunches, flashes of thoughts.

(2) Learn to trust new ideas, and be willing to take the risk of introducing them.

(3) Develop a single-mindedness in pursuit of some goal or objective.

(4) Try to establish a balanced view that considers both negative and positive, dark and bright sides, of a situation, problem, or decision.

(5) Develop the willingness to act alone and be alone for some worthwhile project.

(6) Develop the psychic strength to tackle something that looks seemingly impossible.

(7) Show a decisiveness and single-mindedness about some important topic and even about the direction of one's own life.

(8) Work on developing a logical approach that analyzes a situation before making a decision.

(9) Take the responsibility for organizing and seeing to completion some project.

(10) Consider the long term consequences of your actions and decisions.

THE PRAYER OF THE ISFP TYPE
(Basic Temperament = SP)

DOMINANT-Feeling, AUXILIARY-Sensation
INFERIOR-Thinking, TERTIARY-Intuition

The ISFPs are free spirits, who desire to follow the guidance of the Holy Spirit and impulse of the moment. They are capable of a great intensity of feeling and have an eye for detail. Endowed with artistic ability, they are lovers of nature. The beauties of nature speak to them of God, God's power, God's presence, God's beauty, God's goodness, and God's loving care.

At Eucharist ISFPs enjoy good congregational singing, especially folk music. Good experiences of community and a prayerful, enthusiastic, spirit-filled celebrant make their Sunday Mass most profitable and enjoyable. Therefore, a Cursillo Weekend, or membership on a Cursillo Team, is recommended for them. ISFPs will enjoy sharing the fellowship, singing and praising of God, in a prayer group.

Prayer forms for this type need to be flexible to allow the ISFP to go in whatever direction the Spirit leads. However, they must not allow this to prevent them from spending at least one-half hour each day in prayerful reflection to allow a real contact with the Holy Spirit and to put their life in a balanced order. For this to happen, they must maintain discipline in their life especially in giving prime time each day to listening to God in prayerful reflection. The Benedictine *Lectio Divina* of spiritual reading, reflection, prayer, and contemplation will be very helpful in this regard.

ISFPs need to speak to God from the heart regarding whatever they happen to be thinking about or trying to decide. ISFPs must keep their mind and heart open to any new inspirations of the Holy Spirit. Using a daily spiritual journal to communicate with God is an excellent method to maintain this intimate contact with God, the Holy Spirit, and Jesus.

ISFPs can expect experiences of God's presence that are real and deep and sometimes quite awesome. They need assurances of God's personal love for them and normally God is not reluctant to give them a sensible experience of His presence and loving care. God seems to favor them especially with answers to prayers for both inner and bodily healings of self and others. The Baptism of the Holy Spirit, through the laying on of hands by a Prayer Group, sought and devoutly received, is often a very real and vivid experience for ISFPs.

An appropriate Scripture passage for ISFPs would be: "Rejoice in the Lord always! Again I say, rejoice! Let everyone see how unselfish you are. The Lord is near. Dismiss all anxiety from your minds. Present your needs to God in every form of prayer and petitions full of gratitude. Then God's own peace, which is beyond all understanding, will stand guard over your hearts and minds, in Christ Jesus" (Philippians 4:4-7).

ISFPs will find most appealing the Franciscan type of prayer of spontaneous praise and gratitude. However, Ignatian and Augustinian prayer forms, as well as *Lectio Divina*, will also be valuable and useful for them. Only the Thomistic type of prayer will be found difficult; but effort should be made to use this form of prayer when well-rested and lots of leisure time is available. If so used, the transcendent dimension of their Inferior Function will suddenly reveal to them beautiful new insights into divine truth. Thus they are able to simplify what previously had seemed quite confused and complex. Once successfully experienced. Thomistic prayer will also become attractive to them. Their spirituality, because of their artistic and free spirit, may be expressed in some external form of sensible art: music, painting, dance, flower arranging, sculpture.

RECOGNIZING AND DEVELOPING
THE POTENTIAL OF THE ISFP SHADOW

Become familiar with the basic attributes of the ENTJ personality, which is your opposite in type. Consider how you do not use your Inferior Function of Thinking and Tertiary Function of Intuition to the fullest. When reading the portrait of the ENTJ type, what specifically struck you as so different from your customary way of acting and doing? During your period of prayer think about how these new attributes and ways of relating could be manifested in your daily living. Meditate prayerfully on each one of the qualities of the ENTJ that you wish to acquire by using perhaps the Thomistic method of prayerful consideration, asking yourself the questions: what, why, how, when, where, who, with what helps?

The shadow qualities that the ISFP should consider at prayer, ponder upon, and act upon are reflected in some or all of the following suggestions.

(1) Organize and carry through some project. Set goals and objectives ahead of time; prepare a schedule; develop a time frame; and then try to stick to the schedule.

(2) Be persevering and stubborn in following through some project or idea.

(3) Take some task that requires you to work under pressure to meet a deadline.

(4) Endeavor to be logical in analyzing and reasoning.

(5) Make an effort to convince someone who does not agree with you; be willing to disagree; yet stick to your convictions openly as well as silently.

(6) Select a subject for study and persevere until a good grasp of it has been attained.

(7) Start a savings account at the bank.

(8) Seek an opportunity to do public speaking.

(9) Talk about your accomplishments in public as well as in private.

(10) Be willing to be in the limelight or center of attention for a while.

THE PRAYER OF THE ESFJ TYPE
(Basic Temperament = SJ)

DOMINANT-Feeling, AUXILIARY-Sensation
INFERIOR-Thinking, TERTIARY-Intuition

The ESFJ person is the most sociable of all the types. They find it easy to make friends with even total strangers. Sympathetic, their emotions are very close to the surface at all times. Out-going, soft-hearted, sentimental, they need to be loved and noticed and appreciated. They are very giving, caring, comforting. They need and seek harmony and are strongly affected by the opinion of others.

ESFJs love to pray in groups and find prayer groups quite helpful to spiritual growth. A small group, like a Cursillo Group Reunion, with whom they can pray and share and receive, will give support to their spiritual life. Since they love to pray and sing in groups, they usually enjoy charismatic prayer groups with praising, singing, and uninhibited expression of emotions. They do not mind long prayers.

The ESFJ needs to learn to talk to God as if He were a friend. Intercessory prayers for others should form a substantial part of their prayer life. Their needs, problems, their friends, and others in need should be the subject of their conversations with God. Praise, gratitude, humility, and petitions should be present in a proper balance. Using a spiritual journal to write a letter to Jesus each day would be another way for the ESFJ to talk to God.

Since ESFJs have a tendency to do all the talking when in prayer, special effort to learn and practice the skill of "listening" to God should be made. The four parts of *Lectio Divina* would be most helpful in this regard. After some reading of the Scriptures or other religious writings, ESFJs should meditate and reflect upon the lessons therein, seeking to discern God's will for them in the reading; then gratitude, praise, and petition, or resolution and commitment may follow with some quiet time to contemplate and enjoy the goodness of God.

The Scriptures most useful to the ESFJ will be the Psalms, the historical books of the Old Testament, the four Gospels, Acts, Epistle of James, First Epistle of John. ESFJs should be able to put to good use all forms of prayer: Ignatian, Benedictine, Franciscan, Augustinian. Ignatian and Franciscan should be the two favorite forms of prayer for the ESFJ, although some ESFJs have difficulty with the structuring and discipline required for the Ignatian type. The Thomistic type of prayer will require the most effort but can also be very rewarding when one is well-rested and will give it the needed time.

The Jesus Prayer, "Lord Jesus Christ, have mercy on me," may well be a favorite ejaculation that can be repeated many times during the day. The Rosary can also be used profitably by this type. As far as possible the ESFJ should strive to live consciously in God's presence and use spontaneous prayer to evoke this continual presence of a loving God. ESFJs can rather easily center their heart on God and thus remain in the presence of God and prayer all day long.

ESFJs can expect many feelings of joy, peace, happiness while praying and should see these as authentic spiritual experiences of the presence of God in their lives. Apt to experience God through frequent answers to their prayers of intercession, they may also experience an emptiness which alternates with a feeling of closeness to God. Both are true spiritual experiences to remind them of the need of God and their total dependence upon Him. ESFJs should be grateful for every experience of God's presence, support, love, and help.

Recognizing and Developing
The Potential of the ESFJ Shadow

Become familiar with the basic attributes of the INTP personality, which is your opposite in type. Consider how you do not use your Inferior Function of Thinking and Tertiary Function of Intuition to the fullest. When reading the portrait of the INTP type, what specifically struck you as so different from your customary way of acting and doing? During your period of prayer think about how these new attributes and ways of relating could be manifested in your daily living. Meditate prayerfully on each one of the qualities of the INTP that you wish to acquire by using perhaps the Thomistic method of prayerful consideration, asking yourself the questions: what, why, how, when, where, who, with what helps?

The shadow qualities that the ESFJ should consider at prayer, ponder upon, and act upon are reflected in some or all of the following suggestions.

(1) Look on the bright, optimistic side of things rather than only the dark and worst possibilities.

(2) Spend some time alone every day; perhaps make a silent, directed retreat.

(3) Spend some time thinking about your own worth as a person and individual.

(4) Face up to some disagreeable facts about yourself, your family, the community, and the world.

(5) Do some abstract, logical, objective thinking on some subject.

(6) Be willing to disagree openly with someone and even argue over it.

(7) Pursue study of some religious topic until you have full grasp of it.

(8) Make a special effort to be precise in thinking through some topic.

(9) Try to practice flexibility and open-mindedness.

(10) Deviate from your regular routine at home for a whole week or even a whole month.

(11) Be generous. Give to the poor until it hurts.

THE PRAYER OF THE ISFJ TYPE
(Basic Temperament = SJ)

DOMINANT-Sensation, AUXILIARY-Feeling
INFERIOR-Intuition, TERTIARY-Thinking

ISFJs are super-dependable, have a strong sense of duty, and usually relate well to people. They have a good sense of history and continuity and therefore may be conservative by nature. They love to minister to the needs of others and so are often overworked, imposed upon, and taken for granted. Because of their introverted tendency to avoid the limelight, they are often undervalued. Therefore, they are frequently taken advantage of by selfish, unthinking people and not appreciated for what they do.

ISFJs show an intense seriousness of purpose and a great generosity in pursuing whatever goal or ideal they choose. Among those who responded to the Prayer Project, the ISFJs outnumbered any other type of personality. This indicates their desire to want to please God and find the best way of praying to God.

The ISFJ likes to pray alone (introvert) and enjoys silent

THE PRAYER OF THE ENFP TYPE
(Basic Temperament = NF)

DOMINANT-Intuition, AUXILIARY-Feeling
INFERIOR-Sensation, TERTIARY-Thinking

Usually optimistic, ENFPs are warmly enthusiastic, imaginative, non-comformist. Their intuitive powers are quite strong, and they frequently experience Extrasensory Perception (ESP). Warm and sympathetic, they are usually skilled in handling people. Their extraversion tends to be well-developed, as is their attraction to the novel and dramatic.

For ENFPs prayer is a necessity for survival, and they should allocate an hour each day for it. This hour may be spent in any, or all, of the four aspects of *Lectio Divina* spiritual reading of Scripture or other religious books; meditation and reflection on what has been read; prayers of petition, praise, gratitude, or contrition; contemplation on the beauties of God. ENFPs may find it profitable to use the prayers of different biblical personalities: e.g., the Canticles of Moses, Daniel, Mary, Elizabeth, Paul, and Jesus. Isaiah, the Song of Songs, the Psalms, the Gospels (particularly Luke and John), and the Pauline Epistles will speak most to the ENFP in prayerful reflection.

ENFPs need to pray alone; but, more than other temperaments, they need the help of a community or prayer companion in order to pray. Therefore, good community experiences in liturgy are essential if the Eucharist is to be profitable to ENFPs.

ENFPs usually dislike repetitive prayer and find it better to use spontaneous prayer rising from the heart. Being extraverted, there is a tendency for ENFPs to want to do most or all of the talking when at prayer. Therefore, it is important that the ENFP spends at least half of the time listening and trying to discern what God wishes to say to them. ENFPs quite often have deep spiritual experiences of the presence of God or other spiritual presences. Such mystical experiences may occur at the time of prayer, at liturgy, or other times. They may feel a presence which reaches out and touches them or is a partner with them in a celebration of joy and elation. ENFPs need especially to work at developing good skills for interpreting the insights that come to them in prayer or from the words of the Bible. "Be still and listen" should be their motto.

ENFPs may enjoy the Rosary if it is kept flexible to accommodate their different moods and thoughts. However, on the whole, ENFPs often find it difficult to make use of their sensible imagination in prayer. This will expain the problem they have in using the Ignatian Spiritual Exercises. Unless the director modifies them to meet the needs of the ENFP personality, the Thirty Day Spiritual Exercises of St. Ignatius may be too much for them. The Augustinian type of prayer is especially appropriate for the needs of the ENFP personality. ENFPs can take a Scripture Passage and apply it with facility to their own life or the living situation of people in today's world.

ENFPs need to put some structure into their prayer life which otherwise will break down or evaporate. They should set a time-table for completion of projects since they have a propensity for procrastination of anything that is difficult and requires prolonged effort. However, too much structure will inhibit their prayerful union with God, so a proper balance must be struck. ENFPs must take care not to get themselves overloaded with activities; for as a result, they may end up going in circles and accomplishing little or nothing.

Recognizing and Developing
The Potential of the ENFP Shadow

Become familiar with the basic attributes of the ISTJ personality, which is your opposite in type. Consider how you do not use your Inferior Function of Sensing and Tertiary Function of Thinking to the fullest. When reading the portrait of the ISTJ type, what specifically struck you as so different from your customary way of acting and doing? During your period of prayer think about how these new attributes and ways of relating could be manifested in your daily living. Meditate prayerfully on each one of the qualities of the ISTJ that you wish to acquire by using perhaps the Thomistic method of prayerful consideration, asking yourself the questions: what, why, how, when, where, who, with what helps?

The shadow qualities that the ENFP should consider at prayer, ponder upon, and act upon are reflected in some or all of the following suggestions.

(1) Reflect and concentrate more on developing the inner life of the spirit.

(2) Practice self-discipline, self-denial, fasting in some way.

(3) Be realistic, practical, patient with painstaking details.

(4) Deliberately carry out some routine tasks that you hate to do each day.

(5) Be thoroughly systematic in all you do for the next month.

(6) Follow standard operating procedures in some area of your life.

(7) Plan and organize some project, set a schedule for completion, and then follow it through to completion.

(8) Develop a better eye for detail and memory of facts.

(9) Make a deliberate attempt to use logical analysis in solving some problem.

(10) Be open to the ideas of others and willing to forego your own plans in order accomplish some project.

(11) Be patient with those who disagree with you.

(12) Be faithful to your word, promise, commitment; show reliability and stability.

THE PRAYER OF THE INFP TYPE
(Basic Temperament = NF)

DOMINANT-Feeling, AUXILIARY-Intuition
INFERIOR-Thinking, TERTIARY-Sensation

INFPs have a great desire to pray alone and silently. An hour of formal prayer each day, set aside exclusively for God, is a must for INFPs. All four aspects of *Lectio Divina* may be used profitably by the INFP: spiritual reading; reflection on the new insights discovered in this reading; spontaneous prayer of gratitude, humility, petition, etc.; contemplation on the beauties of God or just resting quietly in His presence.

Because of this need of prayer, INFPs are constantly searching for new and better ways of prayer; and most INFPs have been in a prayer group. However, because they are introverted intuitives, flexible and open to new ideas, most of the prayer groups did not fulfill their requirements for prayer. They find that more quiet time than provided by the normal group meeting is essential. Therefore, they usually abandon such groups and seek other more individualistic ways.

INFPs should read short, appropriate passages of the Bible, try to apply them to their situation, and then discern what the Lord is revealing to them in the passage. This is the Augustinian method of prayer. Long passages of Scripture should not be read during prayer. This is appropriate for a devout study of the Bible but not during prayer time. The favorite Books of the Bible for the INFP temperament are: Second Isaiah, the Psalms, the Gospels, and the Pauline Epistles. Once the INFP discovers an appropriate Scripture passage, this may be used again and again during the daily prayer period. The INFP should never be in a hurry to go to the next verse or another Scripture passage but should linger prayerfully over each verse or phrase or word as long as possible.

INFPs usually dislike set forms of prayer and prefer a more personal, spontaneous response to God. INFPs like to look at prayer not as a formal duty but rather as a time of joyful communion with one's most beloved friend: Jesus, or God the Father, or the Holy Spirit. They need to take time just to sit and be still and wait for the Lord to make known His will to them. This will result in experiences of a deep union of love with God and with the whole world.

INFPs can expect to have many close encounters with God during prayer. These faith experiences often bring a warmth of the presence of God into their lives. An over-powering sense of God's loving care may come in times of deep anguish, fear, trouble. A feeling of being carried out of one's self into the arms of God is sometimes experienced by INFPs. Another spiritual experience of INFPs is a feeling of deep attraction to God and a sense of divine providence or the loving and constant care of a merciful God. This leads to a deep trust in God.

INFPs need to be open and receptive to whatever the Lord wants of them. A requisite for them is to take seriously any hunch, intuition, or inspiration that comes to them. These should be submitted to their common sense or to the judgment of a spiritual friend or advisor who is trustworthy. These inspirations will sometimes come by way of dreams. A journal recording their dreams and their spiritual and temporal progression will help the INFP if it is kept unstructured and seen as a way of conversing with God and keeping a record of the new ideas or insights that come while reading, or praying, or just thinking.

Since there is a real danger of the INFP becoming too introverted, too self-centered, INFPs must make a special effort every day to forget themselves and reach out to others. The INFP must not wait until whole and healed before reaching out to heal and help others. The INFP should begin his/her day with: "What can I do today to make others happier and better for having met me?"

Recognizing and Developing The Potential of the INFP Shadow

Become familiar with the basic attributes of the ESTJ personality, which is your opposite in type. Consider how you do not use your Inferior Function of Thinking and Tertiary Function of Sensing to the fullest. When reading the portrait of the ESTJ type, what specifically struck you as so different from your customary way of acting and doing? During your period of prayer think about how these new attributes and ways of relating could be manifested in your daily living. Meditate prayerfully on each one of the qualities of the ESTJ that you wish to acquire by perhaps using the Thomistic method of prayerful consideration, asking yourself the questions: what, why, how, when, where, who, with what helps?

The shadow qualities that the INFP should consider at prayer, ponder upon, and act upon are reflected in some or all of the following suggestions.

(1) Practice logical thinking and rational analysis of a situation in order to discover the unifying symbol or point that is common to all. Do this when well rested and with plenty of leisure time to allow the Inferior Thinking Function to operate.

(2) Use Standard Operating Procedures more often than you are accustomed to do.

(3) Plan and organize some project and personally carry it through to completion.

(4) Be consistent and follow through on a project even when it is no longer interesting.

(5) Be practical, realistic, matter-of-fact, factually-minded, with an eye for detail. Try to remember individual facts and details. Keep in touch with external realities.

(6) Do a good job of some worthwhile task which is very low on the list of your personal priorities, perhaps foregoing something else in which you are more interested.

(7) Be willing to give up your own ideas for the good of others, or at least delay their execution until the time is more suitable and agreeable to others.

(8) Practice some routine details in living that would give pleasure to others.

(9) Be open to interruptions from others even when it seems unnecessary and unimportant.

(10) Be willing to express feelings and even deeply felt emotions.

(11) Be interested in the past as well as in future possibilities.

THE PRAYER OF THE ENFJ TYPE
(Basic Temperament = NF)

DOMINANT-Feeling, AUXILIARY-Intuition
INFERIOR-Thinking, TERTIARY-Sensation

The ENFJ needs to take time each day to pray alone; if at all possible, sixty minutes would be recommended. During this time the ENFJ should develop the habit of spending half of the prayer-time listening to God and trying to discern God's will. All four steps of St. Benedict's *Lectio Divina* should be used: reading, meditation, prayer, contemplation. Once the "listening" has discerned the direction of God's will, spontaneous prayer, spoken from the heart in a conversational manner, should be an important part of the ENFJs response to God's word. This is the **Oratio** of *Lectio Divina*.

The ENFJ needs good experiences of community at Eucharist and other public liturgical services. This will be fostered by good congregational singing and other elements of good liturgy. That the ENFJ become a part of the Cursillo Movement, first by attending a Cursillo Weekend and then by some sort of service on a Cursillo Team, is strongly recommended. The ENFJ may benefit from belonging to a prayer group which meets regularly. This may be the small Group Reunion of three or four like-minded persons, advocated for the Fourth Day by the Cursillo Movement, or a larger prayer group. Whatever the size of the group, more than likely the ENFJ will assume much of the responsibility for its leadership, since the ENFJ is the most natural leader of all sixteen types of personality. Such leadership may be assumed subtly even when someone else is nominal head of the group, or when no one is actually named as head.

ENFJs do not find the Rosary a prayerful experience because of the monotonous repetition. However, some of them find the recitation of the Rosary, or a mantra or ejaculatory prayer, has a soothing and calming effect when they are agitated. ENFJs should use their personal freedom to experiment with different forms of prayer and different reading material until they find the form or material appropriate for the occasion. ENFJs usually have the ability to use many different types of prayer, and they should make good use of this facility. Usually the Augustinian type of prayer will be preferred. However, with a little effort, the ENFJ is usually able to adopt all the other methods of prayer with much spiritual profit. Thomistic prayer will be the most difficult and require the most effort.

ENFJs can expect even dramatic answers to prayer if their

prayer is intense. Some of the experiences noted by ENFJs are: "indescribable peace and joy", "sensation of warmth", "sense of divine presence", "sense of oneness with God". Many ENFJs find that they have been given the charismatic gift of healing of others through the laying-on of hands. ENFJs should be generous in their willingness to use whatever gifts God may have given them. "Nothing is impossible with God" (Lk 1:37). "All things are possible to those who believe" (Mk 9:23).

ENFJs can trust their intuitions, hunches, and sudden ideas which will pop into their minds. They will usually be on target; however they should be submitted to the judgment of their common sense. Because of the ENFJ's immense powers for either good or evil, it is imperative that the ENFJ be most unselfish in serving others. The constant pre-occupation of the ENFJ should be: "How can I do the most good for the most people?"

Recognizing and Developing
The Potential of the ENFJ Shadow

Become familiar with the basic attributes of the ISTP personality, which is your opposite in type. Consider how you do not use your Inferior Function of Thinking and Tertiary Function of Sensing to the fullest. When reading the portrait of the ISTP type, what specifically struck you as so different from your customary way of acting and doing? During your period of prayer think about how these new attributes and ways of relating could be manifested in your daily living. Meditate prayerfully on each one of the qualities of the ISTP that you wish to acquire by using perhaps the Thomistic method of prayerful consideration, asking yourself the questions: what, why, how, when, where, who, with what helps?

The shadow qualities that the ENFJ should consider at prayer, ponder upon, and act upon are reflected in some or all of the following suggestions.

(1) Make a point of remembering and noticing facts and details of places, persons, events. Try to develop an eye for detail, and share this with others. Learn to give good directions to others.

(2) Practice logical analysis of a topic using the Thomistic prayer method.

(3) Make a point of being adaptable, willing to change your plans for the benefit of others.

(4) Keep your schedule open, unplanned, unstructured, unorganized at least one day each week.

(5) Be willing to be a follower doing what others want rather than always assuming the leadership.

(6) Be willing to live with imperfections in yourself and in others; be tolerant of your and their faults.

(7) Practice Franciscan prayer methods, using the beauties of nature to get in touch with the transcendental values of God and spirit.

(8) Practice Thomistic prayer methods to develop logical analysis and thinking.

THE PRAYER OF THE INFJ TYPE
(Basic Temperament = NF)

DOMINANT-Intuition, AUXILIARY-Feeling
INFERIOR-Sensation, TERTIARY-Thinking

Most INFJs have a strong dislike for formal prayer and repetitive prayer; however if they have had good experiences of this type of prayer in a faith-filled community, they can use formal prayer with profit. They have a great need of silence and are attracted to centering prayer and contemplative prayer. INFJs should tithe their waking hours in order to give 10% of their time to God and prayer. A minimum should be an hour.

For the most part, the prayer of the INFJ should be conversational prayer, just speaking to God from the heart as if to a close friend who is really present. However, a good portion of the prayer time should be given to listening and trying to discern God's will. INFJs are especially good at transposing the meaning of Sacred Scripture to today's situation. They are often good at reading the signs of the times and will often see danger ahead that is hidden from others. It is important, however, that the INFJs develop an immense trust in the goodness, love, and care of God. Since the INFJ can see problems and dangers where others remain blind, the INFJs must overcome discouragement through heroic trust in God. St. Therese of Lisieux's "Little Way of Spiritual Childhood" is especially appropriate for the INFJs.

God speaks to the INFJ especially through the Scripture. The favorite books of the Bible for this type are apt to be: Second and Third Isaiah (Chapts. 40-66), Hosea, Psalms with the theme of trust and hope, the Gospels, and the Pauline Epistles. The Augustinian type of prayer, along with the Benedictine *Lectio Divina*, will be the favorite methods of prayer. However, INFJs are usually able to adapt to personal use all types of prayer, making use of their Intuition and Feeling Functions to personalize each prayer form used.

Journal keeping may be a very effective form of prayer for the INFJs since they are usually facile in their ability to choose the right word or metaphor to express the inexpressible truths of God. Symbols and poetic images are especially important to INFJs and allow them to express their creative insights and intuitions.

INFJs, because of their spiritual vision and discernment of things hidden from others, make good counselors, spiritual directors, or soul companions. Because of the drain that such counselling and discernment makes on their inner resources, it is imperative to growth and survival that INFJs spend a good amount of time with God as well as in leisure every day to recharge their spiritual batteries. It is also important that the INFJ gets plenty of physical exercise.

The INFJs are apt to have experiences of God's love and presence which bring new, deep insights into some aspect of religion or Sacred Scripture. They may feel the presence of the Holy Spirit directing their lives and therefore should cultivate a strong devotion to the Holy Spirit in addition to a deep, personal intimacy with Jesus Christ and the Heavenly Father.

INFJs need to develop their imagination by using the Ignatian method of prayer since their shadow side is Sensing and therefore is the faculty that is the least developed in the INFJ.

Recognizing and Developing
The Potential of the INFJ Shadow

Become familiar with the basic attributes of the ESTP personality, which is your opposite in type. Consider how you do not use your Inferior Function of Sensing and Tertiary Function of Thinking to the fullest. When reading the portrait of the ESTP type, what specifically struck you as so different from your customary way of acting and doing? During your period of prayer think about how these new attributes and ways of relating could be manifested in your daily living. Meditate prayerfully on each one of the qualities of the ESTP that you wish to acquire by perhaps using the Thomistic method of prayerful consideration, asking yourself the questions: what, why, how, when, where, who, with what helps?

The shadow qualities that the INFJ should consider at prayer, ponder upon, and act upon are reflected in some or all of the following suggestions.

(1) Develop a broader interest in other people and things.

(2) Be open and adaptable to others and to new events.

(3) Avoid imposing your will on others.

(4) Be tolerant of others, especially those who disagree with you.

(5) Be open, listen to other people's opinions, and give them full consideration.

(6) Avoid hastiness in judgment and decision-making.

(7) Try not to overlook relevant facts and limitations. Recognize opposing factors to one's objectives and seriously consider what to do about them.

(8) Be alert for flaws in your own ideas.

(9) Develop a better eye for details, get facts straight, and try to retain them in memory.

(10) Practice rational and logical analysis of a situation.

(11) Learn to negotiate, compromise, conciliate; learn diplomacy and tact.

(12) Be resourceful in finding solutions to difficult situations and problems.

(13) Avoid being a perfectionist. Learn to live with imperfections and what is less than ideal.

(14) Take off some time without any previous planning (a day, an afternoon or evening), and just do whatever strikes you at the moment—as long as it is not sinful.

(15) Deliberately leave in an unorganized state some not-especially-important area of your life.

(16) Try to enjoy whatever happens without worry, anxiety, or hurry.

THE PRAYER OF THE ENTP TYPE
(Basic Temperament = NT)

DOMINANT-Intuition, AUXILIARY-Thinking
INFERIOR-Sensation, TERTIARY-Feeling

ENTPs need challenges to bring out the best in them. Nonconformists, they love to out-wit the system. ENTPs are ingenious, always sensitive to new possibilities, resourceful, optimistic, enthusiastic, and are often inventors and innovators. Seldom critical, with a good sense of humor that laughs easily and often, they are gregarious.

ENTPs enjoy trying new forms of prayer, especially if they are complex. They love novelty and originality and have a strong dislike for the traditional, standardized, normal ways of doing things, even in prayer and religion, always preferring the new and fresh approach. Very resourceful, the ENTP loves the challenge of finding new ways to pray or conduct a liturgy service. However, the ENTP may become easily discouraged and lose interest when there are no new challenges.

ENTPs are best at spontaneous, improvised prayers and bored with traditional, routine prayers. Therefore, ENTPs need to discipline themselves to spend some time each day in some sort of formal prayer. The *Lectio Divina* of St. Benedict is especially appropriate. Time should be spent in spiritual reading until some new idea or insight is received. Then a substantial part of the prayer-time should be given to reflecting upon this phrase or verse of the Scripture, perhaps using it as a mantra. This is the time to be still and listen to catch any intuitions or inspirations that may come. Prayers of petition, gratitude, praise, humility, resolution, or commitment should follow. Finally some time should be given to quiet contemplation of the new insight or truth just received.

The Books of the Bible especially helpful to ENTPs are the Psalms, Book of Wisdom, Gospel of John, First Epistle of John, Ephesians, Colossians, and Hebrews. If the ENTP is faithful in giving quality time each day to prayer, deep and vivid experiences of the presence of God may be received.

Because of the extraverted qualities of the ENTP, a Cursillo Weekend for a new experience of Christian community is strongly recommended for this type. Prayer Groups, where the practice of healing of spiritual and bodily ills is explored, may also be appealing to the ENTP.

The ENTP might benefit his/her spiritual life by studying the history of spirituality in order to develop a better understanding of other people's responses to, and need of, ritual, ceremony, and tradition. Contemplative prayer may come rather easily to those of this type. Since St. Teresa of Avila was an ENTP, her writings should be read by the ENTP; and an effort should be made to experience the different types of prayer recommended by St. Teresa. This would include intercessory prayer, reflection on the Lord's Prayer, as well as centering prayer and the prayer of quiet.

Thomistic prayer is a necessity for the ENTP. They have a great hunger and need to know and understand. Once they understand, they can usually deal with a situation.

Recognizing and Developing
The Potential of the ENTP Shadow

Become familiar with the basic attributes of the ISFJ personality, which is your opposite in type. Consider how you do not use your Inferior Function of Sensing and Tertiary Function of Feeling to the fullest. When reading the portrait of the ISFJ, what specifically struck you as so different from your customary way of acting and doing? During your period of prayer think about how these new attributes and ways of relating could be manifested in your daily living. Meditate prayerfully on each one of the qualities of the ISFJ that you wish to acquire by using perhaps the Thomistic method of prayerful consideration, asking yourself the questions: what, why, how, when, where, who, with what helps?

The shadow qualities that the ENTP should consider at prayer, ponder upon, and act upon are reflected in some or all of the following suggestions.

(1) Be painstaking, systematic, patient with small details of some project until it is finished.

(2) Develop self-discipline by doing routine jobs at home or at your place of work.

(3) Develop and follow some routine for a whole month.

(4) Prepare thoroughly for some task rather than improvising as you go along.

(5) Be conservative for a change.

(6) Be sympathetic, tactful, kind, genuinely concerned about someone in need of support.

(7) Be of service to someone, and minister to their every need for a week.

(8) Become active in social ministry working with the downtrodden, ministering to their needs and help one of them to attain some sort of fulfillment, perhaps by finding them a new job or a new educational venture.

(9) Be considerate of others and of the welfare of the community.

(10) Follow a routine set by others in the fashion they would do it, especially in an area where you are accustomed to do things differently.

(11) Sacrifice your one-upmanship for a month. Let others do the talking while you listen.

(12) Make a real effort to understand conservative people and their view-point.

THE PRAYER OF THE INTP TYPE
(Basic Temperament = NT)

DOMINANT-Thinking, AUXILIARY-Intuition
INFERIOR-Feeling, TERTIARY-Sensation

With great power of concentration, good memory retention, INTPs prize intelligence and may be somewhat of intellectual snobs. Having a great dislike for small talk, they quickly spot inconsistency in self or in others. This temperament is the architect, the programmer, the philosopher, the mathematician.

INTPs prefer to pray alone. In general, they need a good, logical, coherent prayer form that is in accord with truth; otherwise INTPs are quickly turned off and abandon prayer. The INTP is able to concentrate deeply for long periods of time and needs absolute quiet and the necessary space and privacy to do so. Centering Prayer should be suitable for the INTP, and a few minutes at the beginning of each day should be spent in this practice in order to center the activities of the day upon God and God's will. They absolutely need to set aside some precious time each day for quiet prayer, otherwise they will never get their act together with the Lord. Since contemplative prayer may come rather easily to the INTP, it is recommended that those of this type read the writings of St. Teresa of Avila and practice some of the prayer forms described by St. Teresa.

A variety of prayer forms can be used by the INTP. The Thomistic method of formal meditation and syllogistic reasoning will probably be the most rewarding since it uses both Thinking and Intuition. Ignatian prayer will probably be the most difficult form of prayer for the INTP because of its emphasis on sensible imagination. The INTP is often unable to use imagination in prayer or to construct vivid mental images or pictures. Attention, therefore, should be given instead to the new ideas that suddenly appear and meditation should follow on what message the Lord is giving one through these new insights.

The INTP prefers to work with impersonal ideas and thus can easily become too impersonal even with God, treating God as an object to be studied rather than a person with whom one can relate on intimate terms. The INTPs need to learn how to express their emotions and how to develop more feeling in prayer as well as in relationships with others where they have a tendency to confine their attention to people's motives and reactions.

Probably the most valuable form of prayer for the INTP is

Lectio Divina. After spending some time in spiritual reading, the INTP should try "listening" to God speak to one through the words just read. The INTP should practice being still to listen for any new insights, intuitions, ideas, or inspirations that may come during this quiet time. These should be carefully reflected upon to spot any inconsistency with truth. If these new ideas or inspirations seem to be in accord with truth, they should be taken seriously and steps taken to implement them. This would constitute the second phase of *Lectio Divina*, the **Meditatio** portion, and should be followed by spontaneous prayer of petition, commitment, gratitude, resolution, etc. Finally, some time should be spent in contemplation of what has occurred during the time of prayer.

INTPs should cultivate Franciscan prayer forms in order to develop their feelings and emotions. An effort also should be made to practice Augustinian prayer. Both of these will help the INTP to develop and use the Inferior Function of Feeling. INTPs state that they can get an emotional "high" from Franciscan prayer. They feel God's love for them and realize they are part of God's loving plan for the world.

Since the INTP is good at finding the correct word or words to define and describe a thing, an event, or a situation, the person of the INTP temperament is often good at composing original prayer forms to be used by others.

Recognizing and Developing
The Potential of the INTP Shadow

Become familiar with the basic attributes of the ESFJ personality, which is your opposite in type. Consider how you do not use your Inferior Function of Feeling and Tertiary Function of Sensing to the fullest. When reading the portrait of the ESFJ type, what specifically struck you as so different from your customary way of acting and doing? During your period of prayer think about how these new attributes and ways of relating could be manifested in your daily living. Meditate prayerfully on each one of the qualities of the ESFJ that you wish to acquire by using perhaps the Thomistic method of prayerful consideration, asking yourself the questions: what, why, how, when, where, who, with what helps?

The shadow qualities that the INTP should consider at prayer, ponder upon, and act upon are reflected in some or all of the following suggestions.

(1) Try to radiate warmth and fellowship to others.

(2) Make a special effort to be sociable with everyone for a whole week.

(3) Learn to express your deepest feelings, even risk being sentimental.

(4) Show appreciation every day for what others do; affirm, compliment, praise.

(5) Make a point of being tactful, friendly, sympathetic with someone with whom you do not agree or toward whom you have some dislike.

(6) Attend to the needs of others and do something nice for someone each day.

(7) Try to bring about harmony in a situation where conflict exists.

(8) Make a point of noticing every detail of a room, of a scene, of a person. Develop an eye for detail.

(9) Take time to stop and "smell the roses", using Franciscan type of prayer.

(10) Be practical, realistic, matter-of-fact; use simple words and simple statements to explain something that seems obvious but is not recognized by another.

THE PRAYER OF THE ENTJ TYPE
(Basic Temperament = NT)

DOMINANT-Thinking, AUXILIARY-Intuition
INFERIOR-Feeling, TERTIARY-Sensation

The ENTJ person is known as the commandant, one who is born to lead and one who needs to lead others in order to feel fulfilled. The ENTJ seeks power and competency and is impatient with inefficiency and incompetence. Usually a very good organizer, very outgoing with people, with good intuitions, logical and rational in approach to a problem, the ENTJ wants everything planned, scheduled, structured. They enjoy working on one-two-or five-year plans for themselves and the organizations to which they belong.

ENTJs need good experiences of community at liturgy and prefer congregational singing to other forms of the Mass liturgy. They enjoy leading others in prayer and presiding at liturgies and prayer services. They love to be with people and therefore thoroughly enjoy celebrations "in the park". ENTJs are often attracted to charismatic prayer groups and to singing the praises of God together with others. Because the Feeling Function is their Inferior Function, they need the help of a group or community to activate their feelings and emotions in prayer. Once activated, these feelings become a great help to their experiences of God's presence and love. The Life in the Spirit Seminars are recommended for ENTJs.

ENTJs desire a structured prayer that shows a logical, consistent development leading to a proper conclusion. The Thomistic prayer forms will probably be the most helpful type of prayer for them because of the clear structuring and emphasis on Thinking. They will find recitation of the Rosary boring but may find the Breviary or Divine Office with its structured forms of prayer helpful. ENTJs tend to be impersonal in their prayer life and need to develop their feelings and may find it difficult to pray alone. However, they need to develop regular habits of praying alone. It is strongly suggested that the ENTJ spend a few minutes at the beginning of each day using Centering Prayer to focus attention upon God and God's will for the events of the day. This could be repeated occasionally during the day and again in the evening before retiring.

In addition, the ENTJ needs to set aside a regular time each day for prayer and Scripture reflection. Use of the *Lectio Divina* of St. Benedict should be profitable to the ENTJ. If the *Lectio Divina* method is used, then approximately half the time should be spent in the second part of the exercise, the Meditation and Reflection on the insight received during the spiritual reading. (The facility of the ENTJ to solve complex problems, address complex issues, and come up with creative new ideas can be put to good use during this portion of private prayer.) The Meditation should be followed by prayers of praise and gratitude, resolutions and petitions. At the end of the prayer period, the ENTJ should try to rest for a few minutes in the Lord's presence and wait quietly to see if any new thought or insight comes to mind. Quiet contemplation is needed by the workaholic, all-too-busy ENTJ.

The ENTJ will be aided in his/her efforts to get in touch with God by listening to tapes of religious music while driving in a car or while bathing and dressing. The St. Louis Jesuits "Earthen Vessels" tape, the Weston Abbey tapes, and the Michael Talbot tapes are especially recommended for activating spontaneous praise and gratitude and dialogue with the Holy Spirit.

Frequently the Holy Spirit will give worthwhile insights and inspirations to ENTJs during sleep. Therefore, ENTJs should try to get sufficient rest at night to experience an active dream life that can then be interpreted by their good intuitive ability. "The Lord gives to his beloved in sleep" (Psalm 127:3). The ENTJ can expect experiences of deep spiritual peace and relief from tension or pressure if a period of time is given to God in prayer each day.

Recognizing and Developing
The Potential of the ENTJ Shadow

Become familiar with the basic attributes of the ISFP personality, which is your opposite in type. Consider how you do not use your Inferior Function of Feeling and Tertiary Function of Sensing to the fullest. When reading the portrait of the ISFP type, what specifically struck you as so different from your customary way of acting and doing? During your period of prayer think about how these new attributes and ways of relating could be manifested in your daily living. Meditate prayerfully on each one of the qualities of the ISFP that you wish to acquire by using perhaps the Thomistic method of prayerful consideration, asking yourself the questions: what, why, how, when, where, who, with what helps?

The shadow qualities that the ENTJ should consider at prayer, ponder upon, and act upon are reflected in some or all of the following suggestions.

(1) Develop your own feelings; show warmth and express feelings to others.

(2) Show constant appreciation for the merit and value of others. Make a point of affirming someone every day in some way.

(3) Be very considerate of the feelings of everyone you meet in the course of the day.

(4) Take time to listen to the point of view of others.

(5) Be open-minded, flexible, adaptable.

(6) Be tolerant of the mistakes, limitations, failures of others.

(7) Go for a walk in the woods and use the Franciscan method of prayer employing the sense impressions you perceive.

(8) Enjoy and practice some form of the fine arts (e.g., painting, sculpturing) just for the sake of the art.

(9) Without any previous planning, just take off for the day and do whatever your impulses lead you to do, as long as the actions would not be sinful.

(10) Develop your senses by noticing and remembering route signs and landmarks on your next car trip.

THE PRAYER OF THE INTJ TYPE
(Basic Temperament = NT)

DOMINANT-Intuition, AUXILIARY-Thinking
INFERIOR-Sensation, TERTIARY-Feeling

The INTJ is the most self-confident of all the types. Quite decisive, pragmatic, single-minded, INTJs do not like to be told what to do since they are usually fiercely independent. They are very introspective, dislike small-talk, always in a hurry, stubborn, determined. In their desire to control nature and people, they see themselves as human engineers and are usually very high achievers. They love to brainstorm for new insights, inspirations, ideas. They may appear to be cold, unemotional, reserved, and unable to express or feel emotions. Actually their emotions are both deep and powerful. Their reluctance to express their emotions comes from fear of their inability to control them.

INTJs need much time for private prayer and are usually able to decide what is the best form of prayer for their own needs. The prayer life of the INTJ is apt to be introspective. They may be uncomfortable in public, community prayer and especially in a prayer group. A Cursillo Weekend is strongly recommended to give the INTJ person a good experience of community liturgy and celebration.

The INTJ is a seeker and should experiment with as many different forms of prayer as possible to discover the type of prayer best suited to his/her needs. Keeping a spiritual journal may be found helpful. The Thomistic type of prayer may be the favorite. The *Lectio Divina* of St. Benedict, along with the more traditional Thomistic form of meditation, should be tried. In using *Lectio Divina* care should be taken to give equal time to **Oratio** and **Contemplatio** as to **Meditatio**. The Gospels, especially the Gospel of John, the Psalms, and Isaiah will probably have appeal to this type.

The INTJ needs to spend "quality time" each day in prayer and reflection. An important part of each prayer period would be quieting one's mind and trying to experience the presence of God and listening to God speak in the depths of one's heart. This takes patience, practice, and may be characterized by an absence of any noticeable benefit on many occasions. The INTJ may take the Lord's Prayer and spend half an hour saying each phrase slowly, while stopping and reflecting upon its meaning and the message each word of the phrase has. Such stillness is needed to activate the transcendent dimension of one's Intuition.

Since this type is prone to a deep inner loneliness and a narcissistic concern about him/herself, quality quiet time should be given to prayer each day in order that the INTJ can become more God-centered and less self-centered. Such quiet time will also serve to quiet the anxieties about one's work and responsibilities. Yet, there is a great need for the INTJ to spend him/herself in the service of his/her fellow human beings. The INTJ also needs to learn how to enjoy and gain profit from leisure time without having to make a project of whatever happens to interest them at the moment.

The INTJ has a tendency to make a theoretical study of Scriptures rather than use them as a device for "hearing" or "listening" to God speak to them through these words of the Bible. They must be careful not to treat God merely as an object to study in an impersonal way. Therefore, much effort should be used to develop a close personal relationship with Jesus and the Heavenly Father.

The most difficult forms of prayer for the INTJ will be the Ignatian and the Franciscan types. They should attempt these forms of prayer only when well-rested and with plenty of leisure time. They may not consider Franciscan prayer as truly prayer because of its spontaneity and informality. Their spiritual experiences are usually in the form of peaceful moments of awareness of God and the fullness of joy in the knowledge of God's love for them. Sudden answers to prayers also give them an awareness of God's presence.

Recognizing and Developing
The Potential of the INTJ Shadow

Become familiar with the basic attributes of the ESFP personality, which is your opposite in type. Consider how you do not use your Inferior Function of Sensing and Tertiary Function of Feeling to the fullest. When reading the portrait of the ESFP type, what specifically struck you as so different from your customary way of acting and doing? During your period of prayer think about how these new attributes and ways of relating could be manifested in your daily living. Meditate prayerfully on each one of the qualities of the ESFP that you wish to acquire by using perhaps the Thomistic method of prayerful consideration, asking yourself the questions: what, why, how, when, where, who, with what helps?

The shadow qualities that the INTJ should consider at prayer, ponder upon, and act upon are reflected in some or all of the following suggestions.

(1) Develop an eye for detail, and look for the transcendental qualities of sensible realities.

(2) Listen frequently to good music, with your eyes closed; do nothing else but just enjoy the music; try to experience the beauty therein.

(3) Learn to work better with others.

(4) Be open to the different ways of other temperaments.

(5) Be patient and tolerant with those who disagree with you.

(6) Develop some close friendships which require a good deal of your time and energy.

(7) Be generous in sharing what you have with others, generous to a fault; give without expecting anything in return; share freely with others.

(8) Show respect for someone in authority even though you do not like that person.

(9) Try to resolve some observable conflict among others in the community.

(10) Be willing to revise your ideas, opinions, plans.

(11) Take time to "smell the roses" and enjoy life.

(12) Occasionally act on impulse.

(13) Be willing to waste time, seemingly doing nothing but engaging in small talk or useless conversation.

(14) Learn to work and play better with others.

THE ISFJ AND ESFP TYPES

DOMINANT-SENSATION, AUXILIARY-FEELING
INFERIOR-INTUITION, TERTIARY-THINKING

The task of the Sensation type is to maintain contact with our historical roots. By adding their personal experience of God to the traditional experiences inherited from the past, God and religion come alive and become a living symbol of grace to them. They need to reflect over and over again on the same faith experiences, mulling them over to see how things fit together. By doing this, they see God's loving providence at work in the history of salvation, in Bible history, in the lives of the saints, and in their own life. By the practice of sensible imagination they concretize the past events of the life of Christ and Bible history until they derive some spiritual benefit from the exercise. They should especially try to discern God's loving care or providence in all these events. Being matter of fact and with a need to pin things down, the ISFJs and ESFPs should look for proof of God's wisdom, power, goodness, love, and faithfulness in the events of their own life as well as in the whole history of salvation.

Throughout the day ISFJs and ESFPs need to be open to the voice of the Holy Spirit speaking within the depths of their conscience and also to take seriously any new insights that spontaneously come to their minds, striving to combine them with traditional teachings in order to form an authentic conscience. When conflicts arise between one's personal convictions and traditional doctrine, they should use their Feeling Function to discern which will do the most good and the least harm to everyone concerned. Hypocrisy can occur when one follows an external code of morality directly contrary to one's deepest convictions. For example, it is hypocritical to profess loyalty and obedience to some legality which one knows in one's heart is contrary to common sense and the best interests of everyone concerned.

Franciscan prayer should be their favorite type. This type of prayer should activate the transcendent dimension of their Sensing Function. They need to use their sensible perceptions of the external world in order to gain deeper insights into the intangible realities of God.

Their Inferior Function of Intuition may be their most powerful lifeline to God and grace; therefore, they need to be alert to any new insights. If these intuitions are neglected, they will tend to become negative. However, if this sixth sense of sudden inspiration is taken seriously, it can lead one to marvelous insights concerning God and divine providence. ISFJs and ESFPs should be especially alert for unifying symbols that show harmony and balance in their own life and in the events of history. One will recognize these living symbols when they result in a profound and moving inner experience or feeling of joy, peace, love, and hope.

The Thomistic method of prayer will probably be the most difficult since it utilizes the Inferior and Tertiary Functions. ISFJs and ESFPs should use it only when well-rested, alert, free of outside distractions, and with plenty of leisure time. To neglect this type of prayer would be wrong. During Thomistic prayer, they should look for new insights and flashes of grace which will help them to get a better grasp of some complex issue. This will be accomplished by an insight that unifies and simplifies an otherwise complicated thought process.

The Augustinian method of prayer may also require special effort since it uses the Inferior Function of Intuition. It is essential to spiritual growth to utilize all the types of prayer. Therefore, special effort must be made to find sufficient time in one's daily routine for a period of formal prayer. A minimum of thirty minutes of undistract-ed, alert attention should be devoted to an exercise of formal prayer.

One of the greatest mistakes of these two types is to fill up their day with sensible activities and ignore the deeper, spiritual realities knocking at the doors of their Inferior or Tertiary Functions. To prevent this a well-balanced routine of daily prayer should include exposure each week to all five forms of basic prayer: Benedictine *Lectio Divina*, Ignatian, Augustinian, Thomistic, and Franciscan prayer.

THE ISFP AND ESFJ TYPES

DOMINANT-FEELING, AUXILIARY-SENSATION INFERIOR-THINKING, TERTIARY-INTUITION

These two types of personality usually have some facility with Ignatian, Augustinian, and Franciscan types of prayer, all of which are productive of good faith experiences of God and divine grace and thus bring a great deal of satisfaction when used. For these forms to be of truly lasting value, the important point is to make sure to activate the transcendent dimension of Feeling and Sensation. This means: activate as fully as possible one's feelings of love, awe, reverence, joy, fear, respect toward God; and maintain a proper balance in these personal feelings toward God. The result should be a deep, personal relationship with Jesus and God. The Sensation Function should be used to form appropriate sense images of God and all that belongs to God. Any beautiful or awe-inspiring experience of nature can put these types in touch with God. Use of the sensible imagination should result in many new insights concerning God. These will be expressed by comparisons, analogies, parables, figures of speech, which in turn will become living symbols which give one deep, emotion-filled experiences of God's presence and loving care.

For coming to a deeper understanding of divine reality and then forming a deeper personal relationship with God as Father, Mother, Friend, and Spouse, the Gospel parables will be especially beneficial to both of the above types. By projecting oneself into each of the parables and taking the place of the characters, one may experience first-hand what it must have been and felt like. Each such projection will add a new dimension to the understanding of the parable and how it applies to one's relationship with God and Jesus today. Thus a living symbol of grace and God is experienced, and one is led to a deep, contemplative knowledge and experience of God (cf., Eph 3:14-21).

The most difficult prayer form for the above types will probably be the Thomistic since it requires the use of their Inferior and Tertiary Functions. Therefore, this prayer form should be tackled only when one is well-rested, is full of energy, and is not distracted by a host of other needs and concerns. Thomistic prayer should not be neglected since it is apt to be a gateway to new insights concerning God, our relationship with Him, our relationships with others, and the proper relationship between our conscious ego and our unconscious inner self. For this type of prayer, one needs to activate the transcendent dimension of one's Intuition and one's Thinking to search for some living symbol or comparison which will give a new insight into spiritual realities. One must allow these new insights into divine truth to fill one with a sense of awe, reverence, love, and joy. Even though one may feel overwhelmed by these insights, try to stick with them and not run away in fear. Simply stay quiet and allow yourself to be swept away with the new truth; just like when swimming in the ocean surf, after the wave has passed over one, the sea returns to a sufficient calm to allow one to swim back to shore. By activating the transcendent dimension of their Inferior Thinking Function, these types are often able to cut through a host of complex external details and discern the underlying unity that is present. Thus they are often able to simplify a complex problem or issue not only for themselves but for others as well.

THE ISTP AND ESTJ TYPES

DOMINANT-THINKING, AUXILIARY-SENSATION
INFERIOR-FEELING, TERTIARY-INTUITION

Use Dominant Function of Thinking to experience divine truth. This should be more than a mere intellectual grasp but an experience of a sense of awe, reverence, love, joy, peace as a result of the new insight into truth.

Special effort should be made during prayer to discover and mull over any analogies, comparisons, figures of speech, images, or symbols that either come spontaneously to one's mind or are discovered in the course of one's reading and study. Look for any images that may be pregnant with deeper meaning. A true, living symbol of our faith can be recognized by the profound effect it has on one, moving one deeply with feelings of joy, delight, love, hope, peace, harmony, order. Therefore, one should be constantly on the lookout for unifying symbols or ideas or images that bring together opposing ideas. The parables and paradoxes in the teachings of Jesus in the Gospel are ideal for the prayer and meditation of these two temperaments.

Use the Auxiliary Function of Sensation in order to experience the presence of God, power of God, love and goodness of God in all creation. The Franciscan prayer suggestions should be especially helpful in contacting God and the divine reality of grace by way of sense perceptions.

These types should get plenty of sleep and leisure in order to catch the occasional intuitions, inspirations, insights that rise to the surface of consciousness. These flashes of inspiration should be taken seriously along with any dream images that can be remembered. Try to obtain the help of someone whose Dominant Function is Intuition in order to interpret and understand the meaning of dream images and intuitions.

ISTPs and ESTJs should try to have good group experiences of prayer (e.g., good community liturgies, prayer groups). Because their Inferior Function is Feeling, they need to be caught up by the feelings and values of the group in order to energize their own Feeling Function. Once energized by the group, the Feeling Function becomes a new gateway to experience God and divine grace. It is important that the group be an authentic, God-centered group so that when the activated feelings open the door to the unconscious, the Holy Spirit and the good energies of the Inner Self will influence the person. If the group is evil, the person with the Inferior Function of

Feeling will be just as easily susceptible to evil demons. This is what happened to Germany during the Hitler regime; the Dominant Function of the German nation is Thinking and their Inferior Function is Feeling.

These types should make special effort not to repress feelings but rather to allow them to show even in front of others (for example, tears of joy and sorrow). Even though this will be embarrassing, the raw emotions need to be made conscious. Gradually through such experiences, the feelings will become stable and trustworthy rather than awkward and crude.

The intellect can be employed to convince one of the value of experiencing and expressing feelings and to overcome a cold-fish, ice-in-veins, detached attitude toward others. Good experiences of deep love for other individuals will allow the feelings and emotions connected with love to surface consciously, and one can then admit and accept them.

The Augustinian method of prayer will probably require the most effort since it involves both the Inferior Feeling and Tertiary Intuition. However, special effort should be made to use this type of prayer each week since this form can be a good lifeline to God and divine grace. Lots of time will be needed to activate the transcendent dimension of Feeling and Intuition. If these Functions are neglected, the tendency of these two types is to become quite negative toward self, world, others, and even toward God and divine providence.

The favorite forms of prayer for these types should be either the Ignatian or Franciscan type, along with Benedictine *Lectio Divina*. Some exposure to all methods of prayer is recommended, but the most frequent use should be made of the type that produces the most spiritual fruit.

THE ISTJ AND ESTP TYPES

DOMINANT-SENSATION, AUXILIARY-THINKING
INFERIOR-INTUITION, TERTIARY-FEELING

Sensation types have the task of maintaining contact with our historical roots. They must take seriously any new insights that spontaneously come to their minds as possibly the voice of the Holy Spirit and strive to combine them with traditional truth in order to form an authentic conscience. When conflicts arise between personal convictions and traditional doctrine, their Auxiliary Thinking should be employed in discernment. Hypocrisy is a temptation for this type, so they must take care not to follow externally a code of morality which is contrary to deepest convictions. Each conflict between the external, traditional codes of morality and one's convictions should be boldly faced; and with the help of prayer and the advice of trusted friends who are aware of hidden ramifications, a decision and resolution of the conflict accomplished.

To make God and religion become a living faith, Sensation types have the task of combining their personal experiences of God with the traditional teachings and dogmas inherited from the past. They should reflect over and over on past and present faith experiences mulling them over to see how they fit together. By the practice of sensible imagination, they can concretize the past events of the life of Jesus and the history of salvation until they derive some spiritual benefit from the exercise. Ignatian prayer is the ideal method for this. Being matter of fact with a need to pin things down in a practical way, they should look constantly for proofs of God's wisdom, power, and love to deepen their convictions regarding divine providence, which is probably the most essential aspect of their whole spiritual life.

However, in the long run their Inferior Function of Intuition will constitute their main lifeline to God and grace. They need to be constantly alert to any new insights that spontaneously arise. If these intuitions are neglected and ignored, they will become a negative factor in their lives. If taken seriously, these intuitions can lead to marvelous new insights. They should be especially alert for symbols and images that express the harmony and unity of the whole of reality. These living, unifying symbols of balance and order will be recognized from the profound and moving inner experience of joy, peace, love, and hope that sweeps over one.

Franciscan prayer should be a favorite, especially for the ESTP, and will activate the transcendent dimension of their Sensation Function. The sensible perception of the beauty of the world can lead to many new insights of the intangible realities of God.

The Augustinian method of prayer may be the most difficult since it involves both their Inferior Intuition and their Tertiary Feeling; however, it is needed for a balanced development of their spiritual life. Therefore, it should not be neglected but used when one is well-rested, alert, undistracted, and with leisure time to give to it. Personalizing verses of the Bible so that they can become a direct message from God will greatly enrich their prayer life and their relationship with God.

The Thomistic method of prayer may also be found difficult since it requires the use of the Inferior Function of Intuition.

However, since Thinking is the Auxiliary Function, this can be called upon to help experience new insights into the traditional doctrines of the Church and teachings of Scripture. These new insights should be jotted down on paper, otherwise they may be forgotten.

One great danger to the Sensation types is their aptness to fill up their day with external activities and to become totally unaware of the deeper, spiritual realities which keep knocking at the doors of their Tertiary and Inferior Functions. They should take seriously any images that come to them during dreams or even in imagination. Someone whose Dominant Function is Intuition can help interpret the symbols of their dreams. These types should be willing to waste time during prayer and leisure moments of the day to dwell on any images, analogies, comparisons, and figures of speech that come to their attention spontaneously or through reading or other activities.

THE INFJ AND ENFP TYPES

DOMINANT-INTUITION, AUXILIARY-FEELING
INFERIOR-SENSATION, TERTIARY-THINKING

These types will favor the Augustinian prayer form which uses Intuition and Feeling. Since they enjoy transposing the words of the Bible to their own personal situation, Augustinian prayer will be most often used as it will be their easiest and quickest doorway to God and divine grace. The more they can personalize a scripture passage so that it applies to themselves, the more impact it will have for them. Since their Intuition is the most highly developed of their four functions, they will be open to any new insights about God and prayer that suddenly come to them; usually these can be trusted as being authentic.

They will be attracted to the future dimensions of liturgy and prayer and are able to recognize and use living symbols in prayer and liturgy. The prophetic books of the Bible will hold a special interest since these types are future-oriented and are always looking for new possibilities and discerning the hidden potential for future good. They will be among the first who stop going to liturgies or stop praying when no longer challenged by routine, worn-out, dead symbols of traditional practices of prayer — hence, the importance of using the transcendent dimension of their Intuition to discern and lay hold of any new insights that arise from the unconscious. By use of creative imagination they should be able, with time and effort, to discover the living symbols of God and religion that speak to people today. Thus they are able not only to benefit their personal prayer life but also can be a great help in suggesting appropriate symbols for use in community prayer and liturgy for others.

With Feeling as their Auxiliary Function, persons and personal relationships are very high on the list of priorities for these two types. The person of Jesus should be the focal point of their prayer life, and they should strive to form a very deep and intimate relationship of love with Jesus. Similarly, the lives of other Biblical persons, like Mary, Peter, Paul, Moses, etc., should be a frequent topic of their reflection. Reading and reflecting on biographies of saints and other mature persons who have lived in the past or who are living today can form a part of the prayer of these types of personality.

Since their Tertiary Function is Thinking, they will probably find the Thomistic method of prayer somewhat taxing and tedious. Therefore, this form should be tackled only when they are well-rested and have leisure and psychic energy to devote to it. However, if they can take the time and trouble, they will find that Thomistic prayer can become an open doorway to God and divine grace. By a combination of Intuition and Thinking, they will find themselves suddenly enlightened with new insights into spiritual realities and divine truth. These inspirations will suddenly appear out of nowhere without any previous process of reasoning. However, without the many hours of homework previously spent in reading and thinking about God, these new insights would probably never have happened. If they had occurred, no attention would have been paid to them and these thoughts would have been repressed back into the unconscious.

These types need to spend time with Franciscan prayer to activate the transcendent dimension of their Inferior Sensing. They need to cultivate an appreciation of beauty, art forms, dance, music, drama, fiction to discover appropriate images, comparisons, analogies, symbols to express spiritual realities. The Franciscan form of prayer is the ideal method to accomplish this.

Ignatian prayer, since it uses their Inferior and Tertiary Functions, may be the most difficult. Therefore, it should be used only when one is well-rested, alert, and with sufficient time to spend in developing it. If then practiced, it can become a doorway to new images concerning spiritual realities and relationships. Before using Ignatian prayer forms, it is recommended that Thomistic prayer be used for a while to activate the transcendent dimension of the Auxiliary and Tertiary Functions. Jung claims that it is unwise to tackle our Inferior Function head-on but rather it should be approached by way of our Auxiliary and Tertiary Functions.

Since these types, because of their Inferior Sensation Function, have difficulty learning anything that involves their senses, they are apt to be disturbed by anything that deviates from the set pattern. Yet, their Dominant Function of Intuition fights against this. For them, liturgy becomes very dull unless the celebrant is able to add some new personal dimensions with each Mass, e.g., through the homily, or music, or the way prayers are recited; but the liturgy still has to be within the boundaries of the proper order which they have learned and now anticipate. Again, their Intuition, which gives them a lack of appreciation for anything that is rote, causes them to dislike the Rosary. Yet, if they would practice meditation with the Rosary, their Inferior Function of Sensation could be activated and their Dominant Intuition served.

THE INFP AND ENFJ TYPES

DOMINANT-FEELING, AUXILIARY-INTUITION
INFERIOR-THINKING, TERTIARY-SENSATION

The easiest forms of prayer for these two types will be those of gratitude and praise and the Augustinian forms of prayer by which one interprets the Biblical passage as being a personal message from God to us today. These forms of prayer will be easy, profitable, and enjoyable because they use the Dominant and Auxiliary Functions. Therefore, they will be the "old reliables" which will carry the main burden of one's prayer life. Actually these forms of prayer energize and open these temperaments to a deep, beautiful intimacy with God.

These two temperaments are among the most independent of the sixteen types. Therefore, they should be encouraged to seek and find their own unique, personal methods of prayer which best enable them to make contact with God and to experience His presence. Moreover, once they have succeeded in having good experiences of prayer, they usually are able to become good teachers or spiritual guides to help other, less creative types to find appropriate ways of prayer. These are the attributes of their Auxiliary Function of Intuition.

The INFP and ENFJ favor prayer forms that deal with persons rather than with abstract ideas. They are able to simplify prayer forms and establish the proper order and relationships between the different types of prayer; but they have a strong bias against abstract thinking and hesitate to face up to questioning thoughts since usually they are not good at handling negativity in themselves and others.

This is due to the fact that Thinking is their Inferior Function. Therefore they need to develop a deep trust in God's loving care and providence by frequently reflecting during prayer on God's wisdom, power, goodness, love, and promises of mercy and forgiveness.

For them, the Thomistic form of prayer will require the greatest outlay of psychic energy and therefore should be used only when they are well-rested, alert, and are free from outside distractions. When used under these conditions, Thomistic prayer will prove very valuable in helping them to perceive the underlying unity of the diverse spiritual realities. They will then be able to cut through complex situations and discern some simple issue around which to rally the diverse elements. Such insights result from a combined use of the transcendent dimension of the Thinking and Intuition Functions. This will prove invaluable not only for their own growth toward wholeness but also for teaching, directing, and counselling others.

Franciscan forms of prayer may also be used even though these too take special effort and may seem at times to be a waste of valuable time. Nevertheless, it is essential to the spiritual growth of these two types that they activate the transcendent dimension of their Sensation Function and use this way to gain entry into the world of spiritual realities. They must be careful not to hurry the process but must have the patience to wait until the Self succeeds in breaking through the barrier that the Ego has erected between conscious external realities and the world of spiritual realities. The Holy Spirit and the inner Self have their own time schedule; and if we are patient, the transcendent dimension of the Tertiary and Inferior Functions will finally open the doorway of our inner being and to the inner spiritual reality to be found in all created things. Some of the ways of activating the transcendent dimension of Sensation are: listening to good music; watching or reading good drama; reading good dramatic fiction; studying or working in some medium of the fine arts, such as painting, sculpture, woodcarving, etc. Using one's hands to work in the soil (gardening, especially growing flowers) or with other materials (clay, wood, paint) also helps to unlock the transcendent dimension of the Inferior and Tertiary Functions.

The Ignatian method of prayer which makes good use of sensible imagination may be difficult for the INFPs and ENFJs since it requires the use of the Inferior and Tertiary Functions. However, with patient endurance and practice, this method of prayer will also become the doorway to new and deeper experiences of divine realities.

THE INTJ AND ENTP TYPES

DOMINANT-INTUITION, AUXILIARY-THINKING
INFERIOR-SENSATION, TERTIARY-FEELING

Since Intuition is the Dominant Function, growth in prayer, wholeness, and holiness will proceed from it. These types should endeavor to activate the transcendent dimension of their Intuition, which is their creative imagination and which is the main symbol-making function of the human psyche. Just as St. Thomas was able to collate and put order into the traditional knowledge of the past and then unite it with the new insights and symbols that he had discovered, so the INTJ and the ENTP can do the same thing today. With their sense of history and their openness to discerning new, living symbols of God and spiritual realities, they are well suited for the task of uniting all that is good in the old with all that is good in the new. However, this will not happen if they repress the transcendent dimension of their Dominant Intuition. As innovators, they can expect to experience opposition and even persecution from traditionalists and conservatives who cling to the old symbols of faith long after they have lost their relevance. Therefore, courage, detachment from self-interest, and a deep intimacy with God, such as St. Thomas Aquinas had, are necessary.

These types should find the Thomistic forms of prayer most in keeping with their temperament. They will enjoy indulging in lengthy abstract thinking about both old and new ideas about God and spiritual realities. They will be interested in the historical dimension of religion and scripture. The danger is that their prayer life will become more a study than a real encounter with the living God as He exists today. They want to put God and the whole of reality into neat "pigeon holes" and unchangeable categories. They favor the **Lectio** and **Meditatio** of *Lectio Divina* and tend to neglect the **Oratio** and **Contemplatio**. Study and reflection on the life and writings of Saint Thomas Aquinas would help these types maintain a proper balance in their life and prayers.

To attain a balanced and intimate relationship with God, the Augustinian, Franciscan, and Ignatian forms of prayer need to be practiced. This will require some effort and involve such an outlay of psychic energy that one will be tempted to bypass these forms of prayer. To do so would result in tragedy to one's spiritual life and probable frustration of the life's work entrusted to one by divine providence. Probably the place to start would be to develop a facility with Ignatian prayer forms, since for these types projecting themselves back into Biblical times and events may be easier than approaching them in another way. To make the Ignatian Spiritual Exercises a real prayer, care must be taken to follow Ignatius' advice "to draw some fruit and benefit" from each contemplation. Also, special effort should be made to complete the colloquy with Jesus and God the Father recommended for the end of each spiritual exercise.

After developing some proficiency in the Spiritual Exercises of St. Ignatius, the next prayer form for these types to approach should be the Augustinian, which makes good use of Intuition, their Dominant Function. The transcendent dimension of creative imagination needs to be exercised to imagine what personal meaning the words of Scripture might have for one today. We must convince ourselves that the words of the Bible are eternal wisdom applicable to our situation today. Using Intuition, we try to discern what meaning these ancient words might have. What challenges do they offer us? The more we can personalize the Scripture message, the more fruitful will be the Augustinian type of prayer.

Probably the most difficult form of prayer for these types will be the Franciscan since it requires active use of the Inferior and Tertiary Functions. Therefore, much time, leisure, and extra psychic energy need to be given to make Franciscan prayer forms meaningful. To reach wholeness and balance, to attain deep intimacy with God, this form of prayer is an excellent means.

THE INTP AND ENTJ TYPES

DOMINANT-THINKING, AUXILIARY-INTUITION
INFERIOR-FEELING, TERTIARY-SENSATION

The INTP and the ENTJ should use their Dominant Function of Thinking to experience divine truth not only through an intellectual grasp but also through a sense of awe, reverence, joy, love, peace as a result of the new insights into truth which they are able to grasp. They should try to experience this truth with their heart as well as with their head. The Thomistic type of prayer, along with the Benedictine *Lectio Divina*, will be their preferred forms of prayer since they appeal to the Thinking (Dominant) and Intuition (Auxiliary) Functions.

Since their Auxiliary is Intuition, they should endeavor to catch the insights, inspirations, and intuitions that suddenly occur in the course of daily activities as well as during the time of formal prayer. Attention should be given to the interpretation of dream symbols and other images that come during fantasy or waking hours. None of these images should be represed but rather an attempt should be made to find an authentic meaning for each of them. The task of their conscious mind and will is to put them to good use in their active life of social service to others.

Augustinian prayer forms will be helpful in activating the transcendent dimension of Intuition and Feeling in order to make contact with God and grace. Poetry, music, drama, and art are also useful in opening the door to the world of spiritual realities. Both direct participation in these arts and enjoyment of them as a spectator can be an excellent preparation for prayer and experiences of the reality and presence of God.

Franciscan prayer forms should be especially helpful in activating the Tertiary Function of Sensation. Effort must be made to go beyond a mere intellectual appreciation of the beauty and form of sense experience. Use the imagination to develop suitable images, analogies, comparisons with spiritual realities and thus make contact with God and spiritual realities.

The above types should seek good group experiences of prayer, e.g., good community liturgies, prayer groups. Because their Inferior Function is Feeling, being caught up by the feelings and values of the group will energize their own Feeling Function. Once activated by the group, the Feeling Function becomes a new gateway to experiences of God and divine grace. It is important that the group be an authentic, God-centered group so that when the activated feelings open the door of the unconscious, the Holy Spirit and the good energies of the inner Self will influence the person. If the group is evil, the person with the Inferior Function of Feeling can become susceptible to evil demons. A prime example of this is Adolph Hitler.

INTPs and ENTJs should make special efforts not to repress their feelings but to allow them to show, especially in front of at least one other trustworthy person. Even though this may be embarrassing, the raw emotions need to be made conscious. Gradually through such expressions of feeling, their Feeling Function will become stable and trustworthy rather than awkward and primitive.

When using Thomistic and Benedictine forms of prayer, the activation of the Feeling Function is necessary. The colloquies and personal applications should be lengthened. In *Lectio Divina* sufficient time should be given to the third and fourth steps of **Oratio** and **Contemplatio**, one must be careful not to give all the time to the first and second steps of **Lectio** and **Meditatio** as these types are wont to do.

Efforts must be made to overcome impersonal, detached attitudes toward others. One may use the intellect to convince oneself of the value of feelings. Then try to have good experiences of deep personal love for others and allow the emotions connected with love to surface consciously and be acknowledged. Such experiences will open one to similar experiences of love with God and the Lord Jesus Christ.

These types need to make a concerted effort to develop both their imagination (Sensation Function) and their feelings and emotions (their Inferior Function). If these are properly developed, they will find their prayer life and relationship with God greatly enriched.

APPENDIX III

A GLOSSARY OF TERMS

AUXILIARY FUNCTION: the second most developed of the four psychological functions. It serves as the auxiliary or helper to the dominant or superior function in conscious activity.

CHARISMATIC PRAYER: a special type of prayer which has been developed in recent years in charismatic prayer groups among both Catholics and other Christians. Primarily prayers of praise and gratitude to God, it usually includes praying in tongues and prayers of prophecy and healing. The emphasis is upon "praying in the Spirit", which refers to putting oneself completely in the hands of the Holy Spirit and allowing the Spirit to use our tongues and bodies and minds.

CONSCIOUS FACULTIES: the intellect, will, imagination, memory, feeling, five bodily senses, or all those powers or abilities of which one is conscious and can use consciously.

CREATIVE IMAGINATION: the faculty to create new images and symbols that will express some spiritual truth which otherwise could not be clearly understood. Primarily the work of the Intuitive Function, one's creative imagination works best when all four psychological functions are working at a transcendent level. The parables and images used by Jesus are examples of the creative imagination at work striving to explain the mysteries of God.

CURSILLO: short term for *Cursillo de Christianadod*, "a little course in Christianity", an apostolic movement developed in Spain in 1947 and quite popular in most Catholic dioceses in this country, as well as in many Episocpal, Lutheran, and other Christian churches. It begins with an intensive three day Weekend, which is a combination of study, prayer, and community experiences, conducted by a team of trained lay persons, religious, and clergy. Two of the techniques used to build upon the Weekend experience are the weekly Group Reunion and the monthly Ultreya. For more details,

181

consult your local church or write the national headquarters: National Cursillo Center, P. O. Box 210226, Dallas, TX 75211.

DOMINANT FUNCTION: the psychological function which is most developed and easiest to use and therefore is the most preferred way one operates in conscious life.

EGO: the "I" of one's life, the focal point of consciousness around which cluster all the conscious faculties. It is the center of one's conscious life as contrasted with the Self which is the focal point of one's unconscious being. The ego has the responsibility for directing our conscious life. To do a good job of this, the ego needs to be in contact with the inner Self and maintain a balanced tension with the Self. In a mature person the Self will be the true center of both conscious and unconscious life.

EXTRAVERSION: the habitual attitude of those persons whose life is centered outside themselves on other persons and external events or things. These persons and things are the prime source of energy for the extraverted person. The extravert functions best when relating objectively with other people and things.

FEELING FUNCTION: the psychological function that makes judgments and decisions based on the value to the persons involved. A feeling person is one who is primarily concerned about the effect an action or decision will have on all the persons involved. The Feeling Function is used to develop personal relationships with other people and with God. These relationships may be either positive (love) relationships or negative (hate) relationships.

INFERIOR FUNCTION: the psychological function which is the least developed and least used. Because it requires the most psychic energy when used, it is avoided when one is tired or preoccupied. Always the opposite of the conscious Dominant Function, the Inferior Function, as determined by the MBTI, will be the Dominant Function of one's unconscious since the unconscious is the opposite of one's consciousness.

INTERCESSORY PRAYER: prayer of petition where we ask God to grant us some favor. For some people this is practically the only form of prayer that they use, which of course is a mistake. Praise, gratitude, and contrition—as well as meditation, contemplation, and reflection on God and the truths of God—should also be a part of our prayer life.

JUDGING (J) ATTITUDE: an attitude one takes toward the world, seeking to control, direct, guide events in the direction one judges best. Instead of being passive in the presence of persons or events, the Judging (J) person seeks to exert an influence on others and on events.

LITURGICAL PRAYER: the official public prayer of a community of believers. For Catholics this is primarily the Eucharist. It also includes the other Sacraments and public prayers of the Church, such as the Divine Office, the Blessing of Palms or Ashes, the Christian Wake, etc.

MBTI: the Myers Briggs Type Indicator, the instrument developed by Katharine C. Briggs and Isabel Briggs Myers to determine one's temperament or personality type.

METANOIA: A Greek word used by New Testament writers to describe the change of direction in one's life required by the Gospel teachings of Jesus. A synonym for "metanoia" would be "conversion." Sometimes translated as "repentance," "reform," "do penance."

MYTH: a story, often enacted in ritual, which expresses in symbolic language a religious or philosophical idea and evokes a response from one's inner being. (See Chapter Nine, para. 2.)

NUMINOUS: anything related to the spiritual (as contrasted with the physical or material) dimensions of reality.

PERCEIVING (P) ATTITUDE: an attitude one takes toward the world by which one remains open and flexible to whatever impression the external world exerts on one. The Perceiving (P) person is more passive than decisive; he/she seeks to gather more data and keep options open as long as possible.

PSYCHE: the Greek word for soul or spirit. In Jungian psychology the personality as a whole is called the psyche. Therefore, it includes both the conscious faculties and the totality of our unconscious life.

PSYCHIC ENERGY: all the power and energy available to a person from one's inner being as well as from one's conscious spiritual faculties. Psychic energy is often used as the psychological synonym for divine grace. It is a grace when used constructively in conscious life; but since it is raw, undifferentiated in the unconscious, it can also be used destructively for evil purposes if one should so chose.

PSYCHOLOGICAL FUNCTIONS: the four ways by which we perceive and judge reality: Sensation and Intuition (the two perceiving functions) and Thinking and Feeling (the two judging functions). The MBTI measures the relative strength of conscious orientation and adaptation of each of these four functions. In each person they are developed to varying degrees and in various combinations and are modified by one's attitude of either extraversion or introversion.

RECONCILING SYMBOL: an image rising out of the unconscious which succeeds in bringing together and uniting two apparently opposite values or truths.

SELF: the ordering and unifying point of the psyche around which coalesces the totality of the unconscious inner being and which in a mature person becomes the central director of one's entire life, both the unconscious and conscious. It is the image of God, implanted at the center of our inner being, according to which our whole nature is directed. It is the point of our inner being and personality that is most closely in touch with God and the Holy Spirit and from which we receive the divine energies of grace.

SENSIBLE IMAGINATION: the faculty of the soul that enables us to form in our mind images of present and past sensory experiences. (For example, we can imagine some scene from childhood or the face of a distant relative or friend.) It is the normal way most people think, and it is done without abstract reasoning.

SENSING FUNCTION (SENSATION): the psychological function whereby we use the five senses of sight, hearing, touch, taste, and smell to receive new knowledge of external reality.

SHADOW: all of those elements of the psyche of which we are presently unconscious. At times Jung used "shadow" and "unconscious" as synonyms for the same reality. We have both a good and evil shadow. The good shadow is the vast potential for good which is waiting to be activated into conscious life and subjected to our conscious will. The evil shadow is the totality of all those faults and evil tendencies in our nature of which we are presently unaware but which nevertheless influence our life.

SYMBOL: an image which attempts to express some aspect of the spiritual dimensions of reality.

TEMPERAMENT: the characteristic or habitual inclination of a person to choose one attitude or one function rather than another as their customary behavior. In this book we have used the term to designate the four temperament or personality types as distinguished by David Kiersey.

TERTIARY FUNCTION: the third function in ascendancy of proficiency and the opposite of the Auxiliary Function. It partakes of many of the same qualities as the Inferior Function in the sense that it is primarily unconscious and can be activated and made fully conscious only with an extra outlay of psychic energy.

THINKING FUNCTION: the psychological function whereby one makes decisions and draws conclusions based primarily on the objective value of a situation as opposed to the Feeling Function which makes its decisions and judgments based on the personal and subjective value.

TRANSCENDENT DIMENSION: that aspect of each of the four psychological functions which is used to make contact with one's inner, unconscious being and with the spiritual dimensions of all reality. The psychological functions are like swinging doors which can be used to relate both to the external, physical world and to the inner, spiritual world. In their transcendent dimension they relate to the spiritual world.

TRANSCENDENT FUNCTION: Jung uses this term to describe the ability of the four psychological functions to discover living reconciling symbols.

TYPE: a group or category of individuals who have common qualities of personality that serve to distinguish and identify them. In this book we use the word "type" when talking about the sixteen different Jungian types as determined by the MBTI, according to the dominant attitudes and functions.

THE UNCONSCIOUS: that vast area of the human psyche (personality, soul, spirit) which is beyond the grasp of our conscious faculties. The unconscious, according to Jungian theory, is divided into the personal unconscious of forgotten or repressed memories of one's past life and the collective unconscious which contains the heritage of images and memories of the whole human race.

VIRTUAL PRAYER: the prayer of action, whereby we express our love, faith, and devotion to God primarily by actions of loving service toward our fellow human beings. The emphasis is upon purity of intention, i.e., keeping the thought and will of God constantly in the forefront of our mind as we go about doing the work of the Lord and serving the needs of our brethren.

VOCAL PRAYER: prayer where we actually speak the words of the prayer. Vocal prayer may be recited aloud or whispered or merely formed with one's lips. In vocal prayer we usually use the words of someone else rather than our own spontaneously formed words. The Rosary is a typical example of vocal prayer, although it is also supposed to be meditative or contemplative prayer by reflection upon one or another of the mysteries of the life of Jesus Christ and Mary.

TYPES AND TEMPERAMENTS
participating in
1982 PRAYER PROJECT

SJ = 133 =   32%

ISTJ	21
ESTJ	16
ISFJ	65
ESFJ	31

SP = 43 =   10.4%

ISTP	9
ESTP	3
ISFP	24
ESFP	7

NT = 44 =   10.6%

INTJ	18
INTP	7
ENTP	8
ENTJ	11

NF = 195 =   47%

INFJ	53
INFP	56
ENFP	50
ENFJ	36

TOTAL NUMBER OF
PARTICIPANTS   =   415

MEN: 115 or 27.7%
WOMEN: 300 or 72.3%

CLERGY: 44
WOMEN RELIGIOUS: 84
LAY PERSONS: 287

BIBLIOGRAPHY

Assagioli, Roberto. *Psychosynthesis.* New York: Viking Press, 1971.

Anonymous. *The Cloud of Unknowing,* ed. William Johnston. Garden City, New York: Doubleday Image Books, 1973.

Anonymous. *The Way of a Pilgrim,* translated by Helen Bácovcin. Garden City City, New York: Doubleday Image Books, 1978.

Augustine, Saint. *The Confessions of St. Augustine,* translated by John K. Ryan. Garden City, New York: Doubleday Image Book, 1960.

Bryant, Christopher. *Prayer and Different Types of People.* Gainesville, Florida: Center for Application of Psychological Type, 1983.

de Mello, Anthony, S.J. *Sadhana: A Way to God.* St. Louis: The Institute of Jesuit Sources, 1979.

Fleming, David J., S. J. *Modern Spiritual Exercises.* Garden City, New York: Doubleday Image Books, 1983.

Grant, W. Harold and Thompson, Magdala and Clarke, Thomas E. *From Image to Likeness.* Ramsey, New Jersey: Paulist Press, 1983.

Hutchinson, Gloria. *Six Ways To Pray From Six Great Saints.* Cincinnati: St. Anthony Messenger Press, 1982.

Jacobi, Jolande. *Complex, Archetype, Symbol: In The Psychology of C. G. Jung.* Princeton: Princeton University Press, 1959.

Jung, Carl Gustav. *Psychological Types.* Princeton: Princeton University Press, 1976.

Jung, Carl Gustav. *Psyche and Symbol*, "Transformation Symbols in the Mass", pp. 148-224. Garden City, New York: Doubleday Anchor Books, 1958.

Kiersey, David and Bates, Marilyn. *Please Understand Me: An Essay on Temperament Styles*. Del Mar, California: Prometheus Nemesis Books, 1978.

Kelsey, Morton. *Myth, History, and Faith: The Remythologizing of Christianity*. New York: Paulist Press, 1974.

Lane, George, S. J. *Christian Spirituality*. Chicago: Loyola University Press, 1984.

Lawrence, Gordon. *People Types and Tiger Stripes*. Gainesville, Florida: Center for Application of Psychological Type, 1979.

Lawrence of the Resurrection, Brother. *The Practice of the Presence of God*, translated by John J. Delaney. Garden City, New York: Doubleday Image Books, 1977.

Meier, John. *Matthew*. Wilmington, Delaware: Michael Glazier, 1980.

Michael, Chester P. and Norrisey, Marie C. *Arise: A Christian Psychology of Love*. Charlottesville, Virginia: The Open Door, Inc., 1981.

Monk of New Clairvaux. *Don't You Belong To Me?*. Ramsey, New Jersey: Paulist Press, 1979.

Myers, Isabel Briggs and Myers, Peter. *Gifts Differing*. Palo Alto, California: Consulting Psychologists Press, 1980.

Myers, Isabel Briggs. *Introduction to Type*. Palo Alto, California: Consulting Psychologists Press, 1980.

Myers, Isabel Briggs. *The Myers-Briggs Type Indicator 1962 Manual*. Palo Alto, California, Consulting Psychologists Press, 1962.

Pennington, M. Basil. *Centering Prayer: Renewing An Ancient Christian Prayer Form.* Garden City, New York: Doubleday and Co., 1980.

Puhl, Louis J. *The Spiritual Exercises of St. Ignatius.* Chicago: Loyola University Press, 1951.

Sanford, John A. *The Kingdom Within.* Philadelphia: J. B. Lippincott, 1970.

Schemel, George J. and Borbely, James A. *Facing Your Type.* Wernersville, Pennsylvania: Typrofile Press, 1982.

Teresa of Avila, Saint. *Interior Castle*, translated by E. Allison Peers. Garden City, New York: Doubleday Image Books, 1961.

Teresa of Avila, Saint. *The Way of Perfection*, translated by E. Allison Peers, Garden City, New York: Doubleday Image Books, 1964.

Therese of Lisieux, Saint. *The Story of A Soul.* Washington: Institute of Carmelite Studies, 1972.

von Franz, Marie-Louise. *Lectures on Jung's Typology*, "The Inferior Function". Irving, Texas: Spring Publications, Inc., 1979.

Welch, John, O. Carm. *Spiritual Pilgrims: Carl Jung and Teresa of Avila.* Ramsey, New Jersey: Paulist Press, 1982.

Whitmont, Edward. *The Symbolic Quest.* Princeton: Princeton University Press, 1969.

A R I S E

A Christian Psychology of Love

by

CHESTER P. MICHAEL AND MARIE C. NORRISEY

The thesis of this book is that the key to a successful, happy life is the fullest possible development of our unlimited potential for love. Much of our energy for love often remains untapped. What is worse, sometimes this same human energy is misdirected and becomes an instrument of hatred, violence and war.

A mature person may be defined as one who has fully actualized his or her capability for love. Maturity, sanctity, wholeness refer to that situation in life where all our energies for love have been released and directed with the right priorities toward the greatest possible development of one's true and inner self, toward other human beings, and toward God.

How we can actualize our capabilities for love and how we can extend this energy in a positive direction are delineated in this book. The insights of the Christian Gospel are masterly combined with those of Carl Gustav Jung to show how Christians should make full use of the psychological tools which scientific research has given to our century.

Paperback, 160 pages, $3.95 per copy. Order from

THE OPEN DOOR, INC.
P.O. Box 855
Charlottesville, VA 22902
(804) 293-5068

Please add $2.00 for postage and handling with each order.
Virginia residents should add a 4% sales tax.
Please enclose check or money order with your order.